# ILLUSTRATED BALLET DICTIONARY

By EVAN JAFFE

Illustrated by PHYLLIS LERNER

HARVEY HOUSE • NEW YORK

*Dedicated to Michael Falotico*
*with special thanks to Gerry Pfaus*

Caligraphy by Elaine Landau

Library of Congress Catalog Card Number 78-73753
Manufactured in the United States of America
ISBN 0-8178-6155-6

Harvey House, Publishers
20 Waterside Plaza, New York, New York 10010

Published in Canada by Fitzhenry and Whiteside, Ltd., Toronto

## HISTORY OF BALLET

The history of ballet really began when the first people jumped for joy after a successful hunt or danced around a fire to pay homage to their gods. The urge to move to a beat or leap and spin to express certain emotions is as ancient as man himself. Ballet is but a refinement of this urge.

Ballet has been called the "poetry of motion." This refers to the ability of the dancer to use the language of ballet to speak to the audience as clearly and as beautifully as a poet might. Since ballet is a highly specialized language, the dancer must first master the technique which has been developed to teach him or her to speak it. This technique is based upon five positions of the feet, rotating the legs outward 90° from the rest of the body, and making the body conform to the straight lines and curves of classical geometry. Using these principles, the dancer can completely control his body, perform the steps and movements of ballet with ease, and use his body as the instrument of expression as a poet uses his words.

But ballet is more than just well trained dancers performing steps. It needs costumes and decor to provide a setting, music to give it rhythm and mood and a choreographer to arrange its language into meaningful phrases. A combination of all these ingredients and the excitement they generate, create a classical ballet.

One last item needs to be discussed before going to the history: the difference between ballet and sports. While ballet can be very athletic and acrobatic, it must go beyond mere physical movement and into the area of expression. The gymnast may execute difficult movements on the parallel bars or the high jumper may leap over a bar set above his head, but the ballet dancer must perform equally demanding physical feats and *say* something at the same time. It is not enough to merely turn or leap. Each movement must tell of love, joy, hate, etc. and be done to the rhythm and mood of the music. While athletes may get many chances during a contest to make a contribution, the ballet dancer must execute his steps successfully the *first* time and make them look easy. The dancer's body is as strong as any athlete's and must be kept in condition every day of his or her career.

Now to the history. In the early part of the fifteenth century, a new movement called the *Renaissance* swept through Europe. Humanity began to think more about itself and its capabilities. The arts began to flourish once again and in Italy, the center of the Renaissance, the art form now called ballet began.

8

At that time the country was a collection of small, individually ruled states. It was customary for the head of each state to provide lavish entertainments for his guests and fellow rulers. It would greatly increase his prestige, each ruler thought, if some new and more spectacular entertainment could be devised under his authority. In this spirit of competition, Lorenzo de Medici invented the "triumph," a spectacle which utilized music, dance, pantomime and poetry, many ingredients of the modern ballet.

These "triumphs" were outdoor entertainment. When the weather turned cold, banquets were developed to provide amusements indoors. One outstanding example of this type of banquet was held in honor of Gian Galeazzo,

Duke of Milan, and his wife in 1489. They were treated to a wonderful parade of characters who danced, sang and read verse in their honor. It is said that the great artist Leonardo da Vinci was responsible for the sets and decor.

As these banquets grew in popularity and complexity, special dance masters were employed to create and supervise the festivities and the first book on dancing was written. More importantly, ballet began to spread to other great courts of Europe, including the French court. There the ambitious Catherine de Medici, wife of Henry II and then Queen of France, decided to do some entertaining of her own. Having witnessed several of the Italian banquets, she wanted to do something even *more* spectacular. She engaged the services of the great violinist Belthasar de Beaujoyeux to assist her. Their crowning achievement came with the creation of the *Comique de la Reine* in 1581.

If the descriptions of the events are true, Beaujoyeux put on quite a show. The banquet (which lasted some six hours) was filled with not only poetry, music and dance, but with some rather amazing special effects including Jupiter posing on a cloud and a solid gold chair that spouted water. What is important to the development of ballet is that Beaujoyeux combined these elements (music, dance, effects) into the telling of a single story — something which had not been done before, but which most ballet does today.

Ballet history changed very little until Louis XIV came to the throne in 1643. An avid dancer, he performed in many of the court ballets. He was responsible for the creation of the *Académie Royale de la Musique et de la Danse* (Royal Academy of Music and Dance) in 1661. This school was designed specifically for the training of dancers. Put in the hands of professionals, the quality of the performances was soon improved, so much so that the King ordered that ballet, once seen only in court, could now be viewed by the public.

Ballet was now in its youth. Still largely a form of entertainment, it was composed mainly of steps from court dances (few of which are still used). But with the arrival of the Royal Académie, ballet began to develop a set technique, an elegant and courtly style and most important, a professional standard. In other words, ballet was evolving into an art.

At that time women were not allowed to perform in ballets and their roles were taken by men dressed in women's clothing who wore masks. In 1681, Jean Lully, director of the Royal Académie produced a ballet in which four women took part. This paved the way for Maria Camargo, a brilliant and lusty dancer, who decided that the heavy costumes of the period were too restricting. She almost singlehandedly engineered an important costume change. She shortened her skirts (to give her legs greater mobility and greater range of steps), wore soft slippers and an undergarment which become the forerunner of modern day tights.

The next great breakthrough for ballet came with the great dancer and choreographer, Jean George Noverre. Born in 1727, he is credited with the development of many principles of dance which still remain valid. He was the first to see ballet as a legitimate art form and not as mere entertainment. Through his efforts, the wearing of masks was eliminated. He was also the creator of the *ballet d'action*, a ballet which told a story through gesture and movement. His ideas and thoughts are set forth in his *Lettres sur la danse et sur les ballets* (Notes on Dance and Ballet) written in 1760.

Most of our discussion has centered on kings and choreographers, and a word should be said about the dancers. The two most prominent male dancers of the time were Gaestro Vestris and his son Auguste, both excellent dancers. Auguste was particularly famous for his wonderful leaps and ability to stay suspended in mid-air. Both, it should be added, had egos to match their dancing ability. Among the women were Maria Camargo, Maria Salle and Anna Heinel.

Soon Carlo Blasis (1795-1878) came upon the scene. To him ballet owes the system of training which was later used by most schools. He also developed the famous position — the *attitude* — which was inspired by the famous statue of Mercury by Bologna. His textbook, called *The Code of the Terpsichore*, was the first of its kind to provide a guide to the training of the dancer.

The stage was now set for one of the most important eras in ballet, the Romantic Era. Beginning with the production of *La Sylphide* in 1832, the era introduced many changes which transformed the art. Women became the dominant figures and began dancing on their toes in what are now called "point shoes." The ballet vocabulary expanded, the steps became more airborne and the choreography became expressive and lyrical. Even the subject matter of the ballets changed. Instead of heroic and mythological themes, fairy tales and folk legends were used and more attention was paid to the decor and music. The costume became the long flowing skirt called "the romantic *tutu*" and the women took on a lighter and more airy appearance. Three women and one ballet are largely responsible for making this period: Maria Taglionis, Fanny Essler and Carlotta Grisi, and the ballet, *Giselle,* produced in 1841.

By this time ballet had reached its adolescence. Born as a form of entertainment in Italy, growing up as an art in France, it soon spread to other countries in Europe, where each added its own national characteristics and style. The Danish developed their brilliant and precise style under the direction of August Bournoville. The English's understated and poetic style surfaced in this century with the Royal Ballet. But it was the Russians who carefully guided ballet to its maturity, and it is to Russia that this history now turns.

Actually, Russia had its Imperial School of Ballet and Imperial Theater as far back as 1738, but these remained unknown to the outside world until 1800. In 1801, Frenchman Charles Didelot, a pupil of Auguste Vestris, came to the Imperial Theater as dance master and teacher. Choreographing some forty works, mostly romantic in nature, he helped to upgrade the quality of dance and training in the country.

With the coming of Frenchman Marius Petipa, Russian ballet quickly rose to international prominence. He came to the Imperial Theater in 1847, became its director fifteen years later and ruled with an iron hand until his retirement in 1903. During this period he created some sixty full length ballets, many of which remain in the repertoire of dance companies today. He is considered to be the father of the classical ballet, that is, a ballet which is based on the classical positions and steps and upon dancing on toe. These ballets also included the *pas de deux,* which the male and female leads dance alone on stage. Petipa believed that choreography should be the most important part of ballet and music should be used only to provide rhythm and accompaniment. *Swan Lake* (Acts I and III), *Sleeping Beauty, Don Quixote* and *The Nutcracker* are just four of Petipa's many creations.

In 1905, Russian choreographer Michel Fokine choreographed his first ballet and the modern era was born. Fokine believed that ballet was beginning to grow dull under certain traditions. Ballet merely "plugged in" certain steps to fit particular music. "New movement should be created to correspond to the subject matter of the ballet and its music," he said. He thought that the *corps de ballet* (chorus dancers) should be a vital part of the ballet and not just background. The most important of his principles and the one which makes his ballets modern was his belief that dancing should be an equal partner with music and decor in a ballet and not only its most outstanding part. His works, *Petrouchka, La Spectre de la Rose* and *Les Sylphides*, reflect these principles and helped to pump fresh blood into the art. But Fokine could not have succeeded to the extent that he did without the assistance of Diaghilev and his company, the *Ballets*

*Russes.*

Serge Diaghilev assembled the greatest dancers, artists and choreographers of his day and welded them together into a company he named *Ballets Russes*. He, more than anyone else, brought the modern concept of ballet as a mixture of dance, music and art into being.

In the middle part of the twentieth century, ballet began to emerge in America. The two most important companies, American Ballet Theater and New York City Ballet, were both established in the early 1940s. But in a world ravaged by war and depression, ballet was not able to make any significant strides in its development until quite recently.

Ballet has finally come of age in America. Now, in the 1970s, fifteen million Americans a year pay to attend the ballet. All over the country ballet companies are popping up, and people young and old are taking dance classes. Productions even appear now on national television. New York City has become the dance capital of the world, possessing both the finest ballet and modern dance companies. George Balanchine of New York City Ballet has become this century's foremost choreographer. His fast and complex style has influenced dance everywhere. This is an age where the male dancer has become prominent again, with Nureyev and Baryshnikov its two greatest stars. It is also an age of show business. The physical and athletic aspects of dance are taking the attention, at least in some people's minds, from artistic and emotional considerations. But it is a time of unparalleled variety. Because of jet travel and television one can see the Royal Ballet from England, the Bolshoi from Russia and American Ballet Theater all in one year. Add to this the popularity of many modern dance groups and one can see just about anything.

The history of ballet is a long and fascinating one, changing with each new generation of composers, artists, dancers and choreographers. But even more remarkable than this, perhaps, is the unchanging tradition which lies beneath.

**Adage, Adagio** — *(ah-DAHZH, ah-DAHZH-ee-o)* Comes from a musical term of the same name, *adage,* and means "movement at ease." The French term, *adage*, is used by the French and English. The Italian term, *adagio*, is preferred by most Americans. In ballet, it has three main meanings. In a general sense, it is any dance which features slow, fluid and continuous movement usually done on one leg with the look of great ease. In the classroom, *adagio* is an exercise done in the same fashion, either in the center floor or at the *barre*, to develop strength, control, sustaining power and the proper ballet line. In every classical ballet, there is a special section called the *pas de deux*, where the lead male and female dancers perform together alone on stage. The *adagio* is one part of this *pas de deux*, the ballerina moving slowly and gracefully while being supported, lifted and carried across the stage by her partner.

17

**Agon** — *Agon* is a ballet made up of an introduction and three parts, choreographed by George Balanchine, with music by Igor Stravinsky. It was first performed at the City Center in New York in 1957. *Agon* is probably the most complex and interesting dance — both musically and choreographically — of our time. Its title comes from the Greek word meaning "contest," and is just that. The dancers are forced to compete not only against themselves but against the difficulties of the movement and music as well. It is a work which tells no story and shows no emotions. What it *does* show is the wonders of the human body and its ability to create beautiful movement on stage.

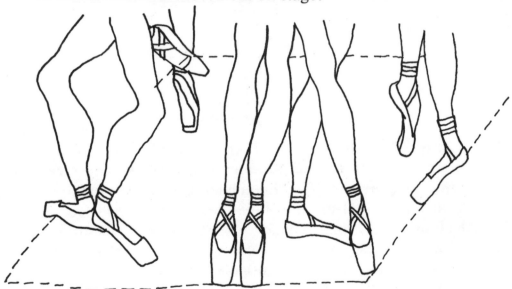

**Alignment or Body Direction** — If dancers were to perform all their movements directly facing the audience, ballet could get very boring. Instead, the dancer imagines that he or she is standing in the middle of a small square, and, by the rules of classical ballet, is allowed to face or move to any of the four corners in any of eight directions, displaying the most complimentary angles of the body. This adds variety and a three-dimensional quality to the dancing.

18

**Allegro** — *(ah-LEH-grow) Allegro* comes from the musical term of the same name. It is a dance or series of steps done to fast music, done in a quick, sharp manner, including many small jumps, beats and turns. In the classroom, it is the exercise which usually follows the *adage* (or slow movement) out on the center floor.

**American Ballet Theater** — American Ballet Theater is one of the world's finest dance companies. It has dance's greatest stars and a balanced repertoire of both standard classics and modern works. The company was originally an outlet for the talented students of the Michael Mordkin School of Ballet. In the summer of 1939, one of its students, Lucia Chase, decided to break away and formed a company called Ballet Theater. From its New York debut in January of 1940, the company, now known as American Ballet Theater (ABT), has enjoyed the talents of the greatest dancers and choreographers of the past several generations. The list of dancers has included: Mikhail Baryshnikov, Erik Bruhn, Rudolf Nureyev, Ivan Nagy, Fernando Bujones, Natalia Makarova, Cynthia Gregory and Gelsey Kirkland, performing works by such diverse choreographers as Jerome Robbins, Agnes De Mille, Anthony Tudor, Michel Fokine, Twyla Tharp, Marius Petipa and others. Still under the direction of Lucia Chase, the company tours throughout the year from its headquarters in New York City.

One of the more interesting aspects of the company in recent years has been the shift from a company which once provided a showcase for new and different dances to one that *now* showcases ballet's greatest stars. In the early 1970s, ABT could boast the works of one hundred major choreographers, with new works introduced each season. Now the repertoire has been limited somewhat, and great dancers have been brought in instead. One recent season featured only *Giselle* and *Swan Lake,* but used a different set of stars each night, allowing the audience to view a different interpretation of the same ballet. However ABT changes in the future, it will remain one of the finest dance companies in America.

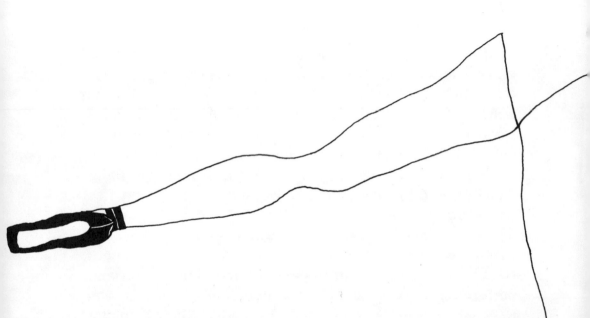

**Arabesque** — *(ah-rah-BESK)* The *arabesque* is certainly one of the most beautiful of all ballet poses. The dancer stands on one leg, and extends the other directly to the back to make the longest possible line from fingers to toes. The extended leg is always straight and well turned out (meaning that the knee of the raised leg must face out to the side). The toes are pointed. The position of the arms, shoulders, head and upper body may vary, depending upon the particular kind of *arabesque* used. The *arabesque* gets its name from an old Moorish ornament of geometric design.

**Arrière, En —** *(ahn-nah-REE-air) En arrière* means "back-ward." It is used to describe any step that moves away from the audience. A *glissade en arrière,* for instance, means a *glissade* which is done moving away from the audience. (see *Glissade.)*

**Assemblé —** *(ah-sawm-BLAY) Assemblé* means to assemble. The dancer brushes one leg off the floor, at the same time pushing off the other leg to jump into the air. The legs are then brought together or assembled in a fifth position and the landing is made in that position in *demi-plié.* The *assemblé* may be done in one spot or moving either to the front, side or back, depending upon which way the leg is brushed. (see *Positions* and *Demi-plié.)*

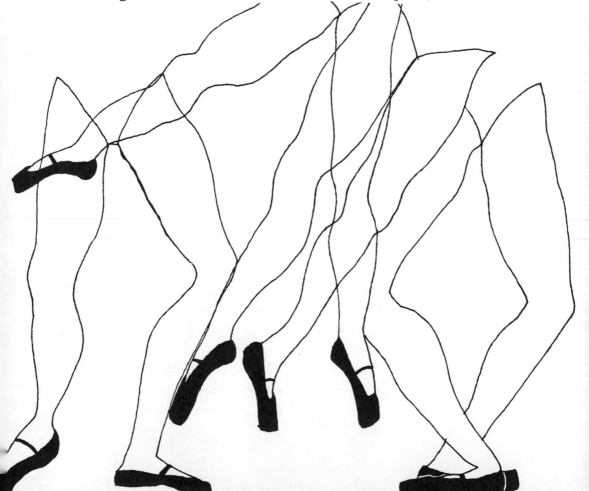

**Attitude** — *(ah-te-TEWD)* A classic ballet pose developed by Carlo Blasis who was inspired by the famous statue of Mercury by Giovanni da Bologna. The dancer stands on one leg, lifting the other to the back and bending the knee at a ninety degree angle. The lifted leg must be turned out so that the knee and foot are on the same level. The arms and upper body may vary, although the arm on the side of the raised leg is usually brought over the head, the other arm extended to the side. The *attitude* may be done to the front and side as well.

22

**Audition** — All dance companies generally choose their dancers from auditions. By an announcement in the trade papers, magazines or posted in dance schools and studios, interested dancers are asked to meet at a particular time and place, ready to show their skills to the director of the company. An audition goes something like this: Upon arrival, the dancers are asked to fill out a form, giving their name, age, height, weight and dance experience. They then proceed into the studio. In groups of five or ten, they perform certain given ballet exercises, similar to those given in daily classes. Suddenly, the room goes quiet. The dancers stand around nervously, watching as the directors glance at the information on the forms and talk among themselves about what they have just seen. After several minutes, they call out the names and numbers of those they feel might best fit the needs of the company. The others are politely sent home. Dancers in general dread auditions but will try again and again, competing sometimes with as many as 150 people, hoping for that day when someone will discover them. To better understand the world of the audition, one should see the hit Broadway show, *A Chorus Line*.

**Avant, En** — *(ahn-VAHN)* A ballet position in which the dancer's body faces directly front to the audience.

# B

**Balancé** — *(bal-un-SA Y) Balancé* means "a rocking step." It is a basic waltz step, made up of three separate movements, usually done smoothly and continuously. These three movements match the three beats of the waltz measure.

In the first movement, the dancer brushes or steps out onto one leg (which I shall call the *first leg*) and transfers the weight of the body onto the *first leg*. The body sinks as the knee bends in a *demi-plié*. At the same time, the second leg is brought behind the *first*. In the second movement, the dancer transfers the weight of the body onto the second leg, rising to *demi* or half *pointe*. In the third, the weight is moved back to the *first* leg. The body again sinks as the knee bends in *demi-plié*. When teaching the step, a teacher will call out, "down-up-down, down-up-down," to help the dancer better understand the motion of the step. (see *Pointe.)*

**Balanchine, George** — George Balanchine is certainly one of the most important and controversial choreographers of our time. He was born in 1904 in St. Petersburg, Russia. He studied ballet at the famous Imperial School, and studied music and composition at the Petrograd Conservatory of Music. At nineteen, he began choreographing and was noticed by the great impresario, Diaghilev, who asked Balanchine to join his company, the Ballets Russes.

He remained with the Ballets Russes even after Diaghilev's death, until the end of 1933, when Lincoln Kirstein asked him to help establish the School of American Ballet and the American Ballet Company. For the next thirteen years, he choreographed for the company, as well as for American Ballet Theater (ABT), and even did some Broadway shows. In 1946, he and Kirstein organized the Ballet Society with Balanchine as its sole artistic director. Two years later the name was changed to New York City Ballet. Ever since the company has been used as a vehicle for Balanchine's talents.

It is difficult to list this man's contribution to the art. He has changed not only the look and style of ballet but also its intent and purpose. He uses generally long-limbed and flexible dancers, trained from their early childhood to perform his difficult choreography. Not based on stories and fancy decor, his ballets exist to display the beauty of the human body (particularly the woman's) in movement and dance. "Ballet should speak for itself," he says, and should be pure and not crowded with feeling and emotion.

Balanchine receives the inspiration for most of his choreography from the music, mostly from the works of modern composer, Igor Stravinsky. He has taken this difficult music and transformed it into beautiful and complicated patterns of movement which explore the possibilities of the dancer. And while Balanchine's ballets have been criticized by some as being too fast, too athletic and without much feeling, Balanchine *must* be considered the most influential choreographer of the twentieth century. Among his greatest works: *Agon, Symphony in C, Midsummer Night's Dream, Stars and Stripes, Jewels, Harlequinade, La Valse, Scotch Symphony* and *Apollo.*

**Ballerina** — *(bal-lah-REE-nah)* Ballerina means a female dancer. It now refers to the highest ranking woman dancer in any ballet company. When there is more than one ballerina on the company roster, the leading ballerina is called the *prima ballerina* or "first ballerina."

**Ballet D'Action** — *(bah-LEY dak-shawn)* Any ballet which tells a story through mime and dance. *Sleeping Beauty, Swan Lake, Giselle* are all examples of *ballet d'action.*

**Ballet Master, Ballet Mistress** — The ballet master or mistress is the person responsible for giving daily class to the dancers of the company, and for supervising rehersals. In France and Russia the ballet master is also in charge of staging ballets. In England and America, this job belongs to the choreographer. The French word for ballet master is *regisseur (re-JIS-soor).*

**Balletomane** — A *balletomane* is a ballet "freak," one who loves and enjoy all aspects of the ballet world.

**Ballon** — *(bah-LOHN) Ballon* means "to bounce." When a dancer is said to have proper *ballon*, it means that he or she is able to do a series of jumping steps in such a way as to look like a bouncing rubber ball. The jumps must have a light and elastic quality. The dancer must spring into the air, remain suspended there for a moment, land softly and rebound into the air again.

**Balloné** — (ba-low-NAY) *Balloné* means "like a bouncing ball." The dancer brushes the first leg out, at the same time rising on the second leg to *pointe* or jumping into the air. The foot of the first leg is then brought sharply to the base of the calf of the second leg and the dancer lands in *demi-plié* in this position. *Balloné* may be done moving to the front, side or back or on a diagonal, depending upon which way the leg is brushed. This step is featured in the solo dance for the ballerina in the first act of *Giselle*. (see *Giselle.)*

**Ballotté** — *(bal-low-TAY) Ballotté* means "tossed." Remaining in one spot, the dancer jumps from one foot to the other, leaning the upper body either forward or back, upon landing from each jump. In the more difficult version of this step, the dancer jumps into the air, bends both knees, and brings the toes of the feet together directly underneath the buttocks. He or she then lands in *demi-plié* on the first leg, extending the second leg to the front. From this position, the dancer goes into the air again, repeats the action and lands on the second leg, the first leg extending to the back. The body leans forward when the leg extends back and vice versa. Giselle and Albrecht do this step when they dance together for the first time in Act I of *Giselle*.

**Barre** — *(BAHR)* The *barre* is a series of exercises done while holding onto a wooden or metal rail attached to the walls of a studio. These exercises comprise the first half hour or so of daily class and are designed to warm up, strengthen and stretch the body, as well as develop the proper alignment and control of the muscles. The dancer usually performs these exercises while standing beside the *barre*, exercising one side of the body at a time. While the order of the exercises may vary, the *barre* usually begins with *grand pliés*, followed by *demi-pliés, grand battements, tendues, dégagés, rond de jambes, adagio, frappés* and stretches. The *barre* is to the dancer what scales are to the pianist.

29

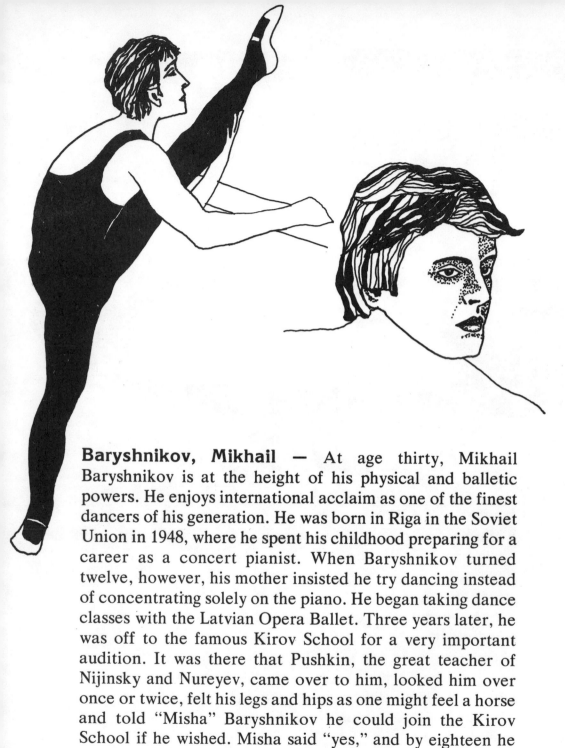

**Baryshnikov, Mikhail** — At age thirty, Mikhail Baryshnikov is at the height of his physical and balletic powers. He enjoys international acclaim as one of the finest dancers of his generation. He was born in Riga in the Soviet Union in 1948, where he spent his childhood preparing for a career as a concert pianist. When Baryshnikov turned twelve, however, his mother insisted he try dancing instead of concentrating solely on the piano. He began taking dance classes with the Latvian Opera Ballet. Three years later, he was off to the famous Kirov School for a very important audition. It was there that Pushkin, the great teacher of Nijinsky and Nureyev, came over to him, looked him over once or twice, felt his legs and hips as one might feel a horse and told "Misha" Baryshnikov he could join the Kirov School if he wished. Misha said "yes," and by eighteen he was one of Russia's most promising dancers.

But Baryshnikov was not satisfied. Because of his height — he is only 5'-6'' — he was considered too short to do many of the classical roles, and he felt the repertoire and choreography were too limited. While his personal needs were met, he still wanted artistic freedom. In 1974, while the Kirov was touring Canada, Baryshnikov — like Nureyev before him — defected and soon came to the United States.

He has become a legend in his own time. He has danced with several companies and worked with any number of choreographers. He has appeared on television and in the popular movie, *The Turning Point*. Just recently Baryshnikov decided to leave American Ballet Theater, where he generally performed, and move to the New York City Ballet.

At first it seems quite tempting to draw comparisons between Baryshnikov and his fellow countryman, Rudolf Nureyev. Both trained in the same school and under the same teacher. Both were stars in Russia and both defected for artistic reasons. But like all great artists, their styles are very different. Baryshnikov is a "natural" dancer who explodes on stage with the greatest of ease, almost as if he were born to dance. He can make the audience feel the danger as he moves into one of his incredible leaps, then lands easily as if on a Sunday stroll. Furthermore, Baryshnikov is famous for his almost unbelievable *préparations*, that is, his ability to leap or seemingly turn from out of nowhere. He can easily adapt to any style or character he wishes to portray.

Nureyev, on the other hand, is a man who lets the audience feel the sweat and effort of his dancing. That is not to say that his dancing is heavy or labored; rather, one is aware and excited by watching the nostrils flare, the face contort and the muscles prepare to spring into action. And while Nureyev is a good actor and can portray different characters and styles, his elegant, animal-like quality is always present.

31

**Battement Dégagé —** *(bat-MAHN day-ga-ZHAY) Batte-*
*ment Dégagé* means "disengaged beating." It is an exercise
done primarily at the *barre* to stretch and strengthen the
toes and ankles. While standing with the legs and feet
together in a closed position (i.e., first or fifth), the dancer
without moving slides one foot along the floor, raises the
foot four inches off the floor and then returns the foot along
the floor to a closed position. This is all done in one
movement. There are several rules to be followed in
*battement dégagé.* The toes of the raised foot must point
toward the floor. The heel must be thrust forward. The leg
is rotated out and the knee is straight. The hips must not
twist and the upper body must not be affected by the
movement of the leg. The leg opens and closes sharply,
causing the legs to rebound off one another. The rebound or
beat is called *battement.* The foot leaving or disengaging
from the floor is called *dégagé. Dégagés* can be done to the
front, side and back.

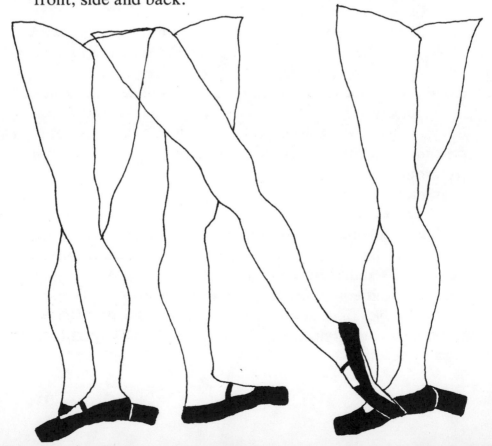

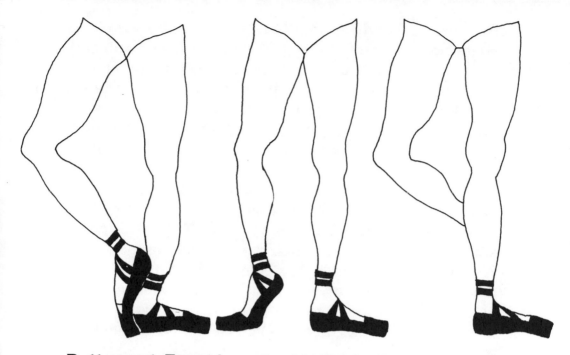

**Battement Frappé** — *(bat-MAHN fra-PAY) Battement frappé* means a "*battement* (beat) struck." It is an exercise done primarily at the *barre* to strengthen the foot and calf muscle for *pointe* work and jumps. *Frappé*, as it is usually called, gets its name from the fact that the foot strikes the floor during the exercise. The step begins with the heel of the foot of one leg resting on the front of the ankle of the other. The lifted or working foot brushes out and the ball of the foot strikes the floor. The foot then rebounds, rising about three inches off the floor as the knee is straightened. The foot in *frappé* must be fully pointed in the open position and slightly relaxed when resting on the ankle. The leg must remain in the extended position for as long as the music allows, quickly returning to and from the ankle. *Frappés* may be done to the front, side and back, the heel resting on the back of the ankle when done to the back. There is also a double *frappé* in which the working heel hits in front and back of the ankle or vice versa before extending. (see *Pointe.)*

**Battement Tendu — *(bat-MAHN taun-DEW)* Battement *tendu*** means "beaten stretch." The dancer stands with both legs together in a closed position and without moving brushes one leg out along the floor until just the tips of the toes are touching, then returns the foot along the floor to the closed position. There are several rules the dancer must observe in doing this exercise. While the leg is extending, the knee must remain straight and the heel must be constantly thrust forward. There must be no weight on the extended leg and the foot must never leave the floor. The upper body is straight and does not move. The legs return to and from the opening position sharply, causing the legs to rebound off one another. The pointing of the foot is called *tendu*, the rebounding action is called *battement*. This exercise may be done to the front, side or back, and is usually done at the *barre* to strengthen the foot and ankle.

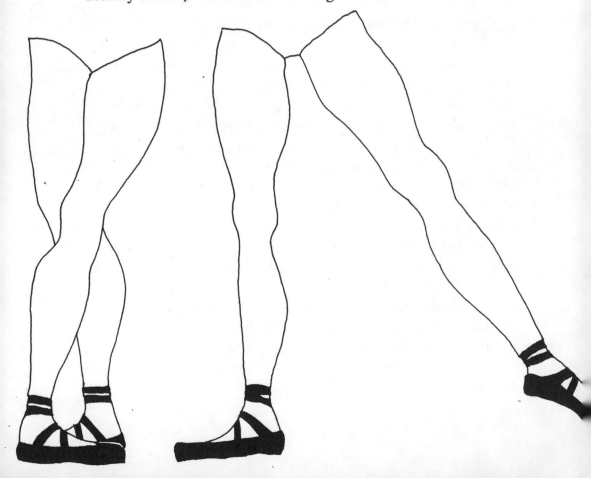

**Batterie** — *(bat-REE) Batterie* refers to all the beaten steps or beats in ballet. The dancer jumps into the air rapidly, hits or beats the legs together before landing. Both legs must be straight and active during the beat. When many beats are done in the air, the dancer's legs resemble the wings of a hummingbird in flight.

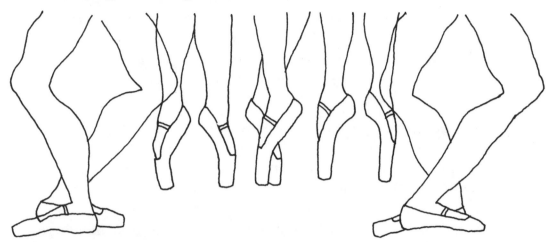

**Billy the Kid** — *Billy the Kid* is a ballet in one act, choreographed in 1938 by Eugene Loring, to the music of American composer, Aaron Copeland. It is a story of the famous outlaw, Billy the Kid, who struck awe and terror in the hearts of his countrymen until he was gunned down in ambush by his former friend, Sheriff Pat Garrett. But the ballet is more than just a story. By using steps of the classical ballet, it attempts to capture the flavor of the Wild West through dance. The men strut about on stage with their hands on their guns and ride imaginary horses. The women in the saloons wave their hips while the pioneer women move more modestly. Before shooting his gun, Billy always executes a classical *pirouette,* but does so in the showy style of a western gunfighter. There is a card game and a roaring gun fight. *Billy the Kid* doesn't only deal with the outlaw, but provides a picture of the land and times in which he played so legendary a role.

**Bolshoi Ballet** — *Bolshoi,* in Russian, means "large," and it is perhaps the most appropriate term for the best known Russian ballet company. The Bolshoi attempts to present new works while still serving the fine traditions of Russian ballet. The company takes dancers from the earliest childhood and trains them in the Bolshoi style — a style which is both acrobatic and highly expressive at the same time. The company has come to America several times and Vladimir Vasiliev and Maya Plisetskaya are two of its most famous dancers.

**Breathing** — Breathing is one of the most important aspects of good dancing. The rule about breathing is very simple, but very difficult to do. The dancer must try to breathe naturally and dance at the same time. While it may seem hard to believe, many dancers — particularly inexperienced ones — will concentrate so much on their dancing that they forget to breathe, resulting in two very serious problems. One, the muscles need oxygen to function properly and tire much too quickly without it. Two, holding the breath makes the body look stiff and lifeless and good dancing must look relaxed and alive.

**Brisé** — *(bree-ZAY) Brisé* means "broken," a small beaten step in which the movement appears broken. Starting in fifth position, the dancer brushes the back leg a few inches off the floor to the side, brings it front and does a beat with the other leg which has come to meet it; the brushed leg then returns to the back before landing in fifth position in *demi-plié.* The *brisé* also may be done the opposite way, with the front leg brushing to the back, beating, and ending front again.

**Brise Volée** — *(bree-ZAY voe-LAY) Brise volée* means "a flying step." At the moment of the jump, the dancer extends one leg, or the *first* leg, to the front, and bringing the second leg to meet it, hits or beats the legs together in the air. The legs change places and the dancer lands on the *first* leg, the second leg extended front. Without stopping, the dancer jumps into the air again and sweeping the second leg to the back, does a beat, changes the position of the legs and lands with the *first* leg extending back. The upper body and arms move forward and back with movement of the legs and the body is usually at a slight angle to the audience. On landing the legs are crossed one in front of the other. This step is done consecutively across the stage by the male dancer in his variation of the *Bluebird pas de deux,* in the ballet *Sleeping Beauty.*

# C

**Cabriole** — *(ca-bree-OLE)* *Cabriole* means "to prance". The dancer brushes the *first* leg into the air. The second leg comes up to meet it. The legs hit or beat in the air, sending the *first* leg higher. The dancer lands on the underneath leg in *demi-plié,* leaving the *first* leg extended. *Cabrioles* may be done with the leg extending either front or back. To make the step more spectacular, the male dancer will often beat the legs together twice before landing.

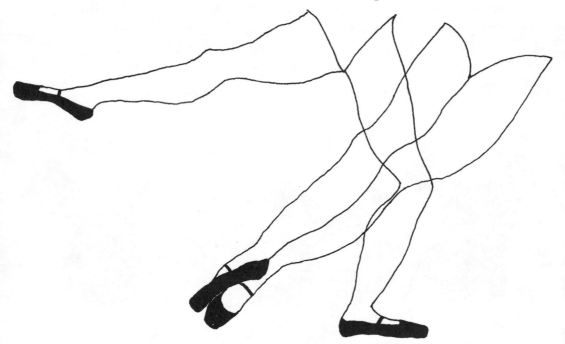

**Cambré** — *(cam-BREY)* *Cambré* means "arched." It includes any exercise, usually done at the *barre,* in which the dancer bends the upper body either forward, side or back from the waist, the head following the movement of the body.

**Center Work** — Any group of ballet exercises done in the center of the studio without the aid of the *barre.* These exercises include: *adagio,* or slow sustained movements;

*pirouettes,* or turns; *allegro,* small, quick jumps; turns across the floor; and *grande allegro,* or big jumps. Center work is always preceded by a thorough workout at the *barre.*

**Chaînés** — *(sha-NAY) Chaînés* means "chains" or "links." *Chaînés tours,* as they are more properly called, are a series of turns done in rapid succession. The dancer stands on *demi-pointe* or full *pointe* (for women) and steps out first on one foot, then the other, doing a half-turn of the body with each step. The feet are held close together in first position. *Chaînés* may be done traveling in a straight line, on the diagonal or in a circle.

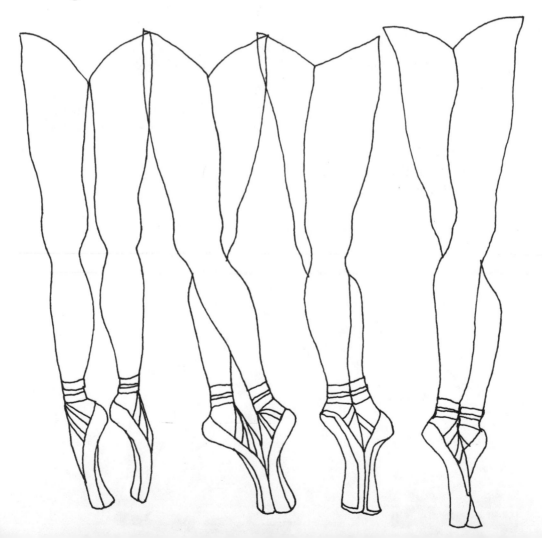

**Changement De Pieds —** *(shanzh-mahn duh pee-AY)*
*Changement,* as it is more commonly called, means a
"change of feet." Starting from fifth position, the feet shoot
into the air, change places and land again in fifth position.
This step may be done as a small *(petit)* or large *(grand)*
jump.

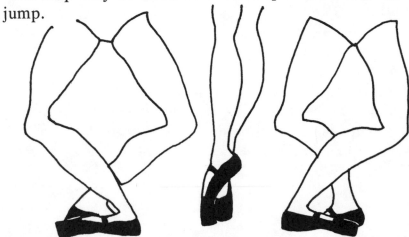

**Chassé —** *(sha-SAY) Chassé* means "to chase." It is nothing
more than a version of the gallop one did as a child. Standing
in fifth position, the dancer slides the *first* foot along the
floor, brings the second foot up to meet it in fifth position in
the air and repeats upon landing, slides the *first* foot along
the floor again. *Chassé* may be done to the front, side, back
or on the diagonal.

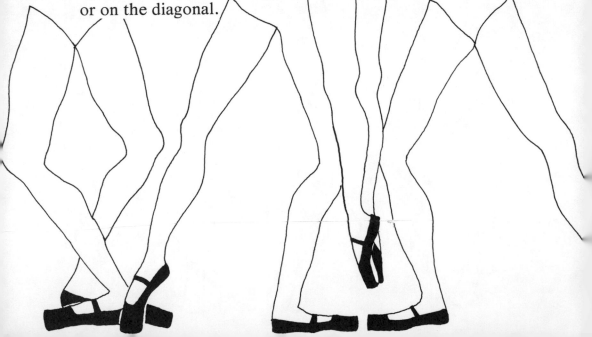

**Choreographer** — As the composer composes music, or the author writes books, the choreographer invents dances. He or she may try to tell a story, portray certain emotions, or just create movement to match the mood or fabric of the music.

**Civic Ballet** — Civic ballet is the name usually given to any of the lesser ballet companies in small cities and towns throughout the country. (See *Regional Ballet*.)

**Class** — Ballet class is one of the most important parts of a dancer's life. As Mikhail Baryshnikov has said, "Great dancers are not born, but made." It is in class that this long hard process takes place. Class is comprised of a series of exercises designed to teach and maintain proper ballet technique, a technique which gives the dancer the necessary strength and body control to dance on stage. Class usually runs an hour and a half in length. The first half hour is devoted to exercises at the *barre*. The remaining time is for exercises out on the center floor. The student is asked to perform these exercises as demonstrated or called out by the teacher. "Corrections" or advice is given during and after each one. Usually, the exercises are done to music, instilling the proper rhythm and "feel" for each step. Classes are generally ranked from beginner to professional. All dancers, no matter their ability, must take classes every day. (see *Barre, Center Work.)*

**Classicism** — Classicism, in ballet, means a tradition of gestures, expressions and steps which have developed over the past four hundred years. It is a style of dancing which is both clean and elegant, but one which many believe lacks feeling. The romantic ballets such as *Giselle* and *La Sylphide* were an attempt to break with this tradition. It is ironic that these ballets, as well as the neoromantic ballets, *Swan Lake* and *Sleeping Beauty*, etc., are now thought of as classical ballets.

**Coda** — The final section of a grand *pas de deux*. (see *Pas de deux*.)

**Corps De Ballet** — *(KOR duh ba-LAY)* Corps de ballet means "the body of the ballet." It is the chorus or ensemble of a ballet company.

**Coupé** — *(koo-PAY)* Coupé means "to cut." It is any movement where the weight of the body is moved by one foot cutting in front or behind the other. It is usually a preparatory step, or a step placed between two larger ones.

**Croisé** — *(krwah-ZAY) Croisé* means "crossed." One of the major body positions, the dancer stands at a 45° angle to the audience with one leg crossed in front of the other, either in front or in back. One arm is raised over the head, the other extended to the side and the head looking over the forward shoulder. (see *Positions.*)

**Croix, En** — *(ahn KRWAH) En croix* means "in the shape of a cross." It is used for an exercise that is done with the leg extending and closing directly to front, then to the side, to the back and again to the side. *Battement tendus,* for example, done in this way would be called *battement tendus en croix.*

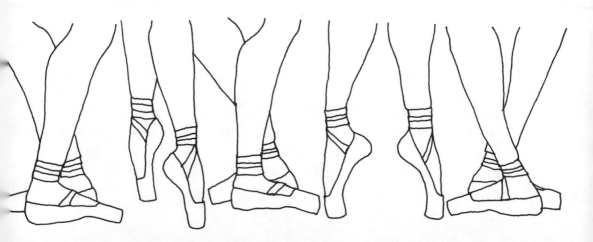

# D

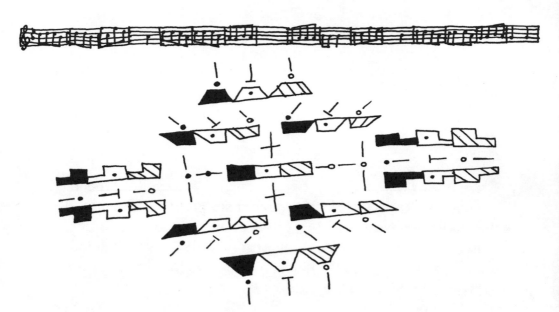

**Dance Notation** — Dance notation is a method used to record on paper all the movements and steps of a dance. Most methods employ stick figures, which are placed either on a musical staff or paired with musical symbols. While primitive forms of dance notation were found in the caves of ancient Egypt, it was not until this century that a truly accurate system was created. *The Rudolf Benesh System of Notation* developed by Benesh in 1955, and *Labanotation* developed by Rudolf Labon in 1928 are the most frequently used.

**Danseur** — *(dahn-SUHR)* A *danseur* is any male ballet dancer.

**Danseur noble** — *(dahn-SUHR NOH-blih) Danseur noble* means "a noble dancer." This term refers to the highest ranking male dancer in any ballet company, one who particularly excels in the classical style.

**Degagé** — *(day-gah-ZHEY) Degagé* means "disengaged." It is used to describe a movement in which the dancer, while standing on one leg, brushes the foot of the other leg off the floor to a height of at least four inches. The extended leg must be straight, and the foot fully pointed. The movement may be done as an exercise at the *barre*, called *battement degagé*, or as a preparation for small jumping and turning actions on the floor during performance. (see *Battement degagé*.)

**DeMille, Agnes** — Agnes DeMille, niece of the great movie producer, Cecil B. DeMille, was born in 1909 and grew up in California. After graduation from U.C.L.A., she began pursuing her dance career. But, as she relates in her book, *Dance To The Piper,* her uneven training, bad physique and late start made it very difficult to get her career off the ground. With much dedication, Ms. DeMille managed to give small dance concerts in the United States and Europe and finally began to receive some recognition. By 1940, her career was in full swing and since then has touched upon nearly every aspect of dance.

While Ms. DeMille has written and performed extensively, her greatest gift to ballet lies in choreography. She has choreographed everything from the classic *Romeo and Juliet* to *Rodeo,* a story about the old west. In addition to working with many ballet companies, she was one of the first to use ballet in the American Broadway musical. Through her choreography, Ms. De Mille has made the language of ballet speak about the spirit, history and character of the American people. Among her most famous works: *Rodeo, Three Virgins and the Devil* and *Fall River Legend.* Her Broadway musicals: *Brigadoon, Oklahoma!, Carousel, Paint Your Wagon* and *Gentlemen Prefer Blondes.*

45

**Demi-Plié** — *(duh-mee plee-AY) Demi-plié* means a "half-bend." The dancer bends the knees slightly, keeping the heels and toes firmly planted on the floor, the back straight and the pelvis level. All ballet steps begin and end with the *demi-plié. (*see *Plié.)*

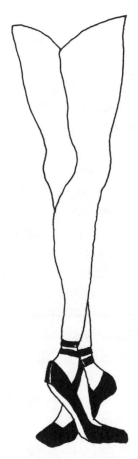

**Demi-Pointe** — *(duh-mee PWENT) Demi-pointe* means "half-point." The dancer stands with the heels lifted slightly off the floor, the weight of the body resting on the balls of the feet and all ten toes. *Demi-pointe* may be done on either one foot or two.

46

**Demi-Seconde Position** — *(duh-mee seh-gawnd poh-zee-SYON) Demi-seconde position* means "half a second position." It is the position of the arms half-way between first and second position. The arms are extended slightly to the side, the hands coming to a point just below the level of the waist and the palms facing slightly toward the floor.

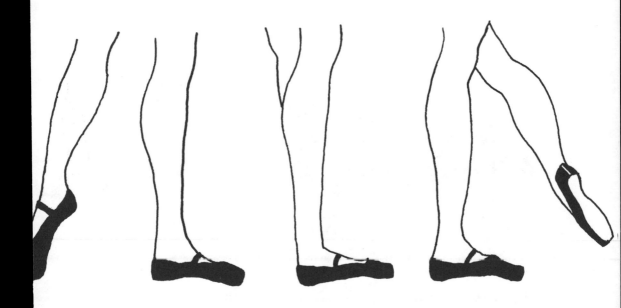

**Derrière** — *(deh-ree-AIR) Derrière* means "behind" or "back." This refers to any position where the leg is extended in back of the body, or at the end of a step when one foot closes behind the other one.

**Dessous** — *(duh-SOO) Dessous* means "under." Any movement or step where the extended leg passes or closes behind the other leg is *dessous*.

**Dessus** — *(duh-SEW) Dessus* means "over." Any movement or step where the extended leg passes or closes in front of the other is *dessus*.

**Devant** — *(duh-VAHN) Devant* means "front." Any position where the leg is extended front, or at the end of a step when the working or extended foot closes in front of the other is *devant*.

**Développé** — *(day-vlaw-PAY) Développé* means "developed." It is when one leg extends or gradually unfolds into the air from a bent position. The dancer stands on two feet and draws one foot up along the side of the other leg until it reaches the level of the knee. The leg and foot then extend or unfold in the air until the knee is straight. In *développé* the foot must stay pointed from the moment it leaves the floor, the heel must be thrust forward, the leg turned out. The knee faces out to the side. The hips must remain level and square to the direction in which the dancer is facing. The leg must hold the fully extended position without moving for as long as the music demands. *Développés* may be done to the front, side or back and are done frequently by the ballerina with the aid of her partner in the *adagio* section of a *pas de deux*.

**Diaghilev, Serge** — *(svair-GAY-ee DYAH-gih-lev)*
Diaghilev was the greatest ballet promoter and manager of his day. Born into a noble family in Russia in 1872, he originally desired to become a composer but was quickly discouraged by musician Rimsky-Korsakov who heard one of Diaghilev's compositions. Diaghilev decided to remain in the art world and took a job with the Imperial Theater supervising opera productions, but his independent manner soon got him fired.

Diaghilev had developed a strong attraction to ballet ever since he first came to St. Petersburg as a young man. With great determination Diaghilev was able to assemble a ballet company which he called the Ballets Russes. It premiered in Paris in 1909. For the next twenty years this company represented the finest ballet company in the world. Nijinsky, Pavlova, Fokine, Stravinsky, Balanchine and Cocteau are but a few of the great dancers, choreographers and composers who worked for him. His genius for bringing these men and women together started a new era for ballet, called the "modern era." His private life and artistic activities caused a great stir among the public and created a most fascinating chapter in the history of ballet. A man of culture and refined taste, Diaghilev died in 1929. (see *Nijinsky, Pavlova, Fokine, Stravinsky, Balanchine.)*

**Don Quixote —** *Don Quixote* is a ballet consisting of five acts, first choreographed by Marius Petipa, with music by Leon Minkus, in 1869. The full length version (which is based upon the Cervantes novel of the same name) is rarely done today although it has been made into a motion picture by Rudolf Nureyev, and is performed in a much altered version by the New York City Ballet. Instead, most dance companies prefer to perform only the *pas de deux* section in the last act. It is a rousing *pas de deux* in which the *danseur* and *ballerina* may display their technical skills in the bold Spanish style.

# E

**Ecarté** — *(ay-kar-TAY)* *Ecarté* means "separated," or "thrown apart." It is one of the eight basic body directions. The dancer stands with the body at a 45° angle to the front. The foot nearest to the audience is extended to the side, either on the floor or in the air. The same arm as the extended leg is raised in a slightly open position, just slightly above the level of the head. The other arm is extended to the side. The head is lifted and turned, the eyes looking into the palm of the raised hand. (see *Positions.)*

**Echappé** — *(ay-sha-PAY)* *Echappé* means "to escape." It is a movement where at the same time, both legs extend from a closed position (feet and legs together) to an open position (feet and legs apart) and back again. It may be done with both legs extending to the side, or one front and the other back. Women spring from the closed position onto full *pointe* then close, while men (called *grand echappé*) jump with both legs together to an open position, land, jump and bring the feet together again. The legs must travel an equal distance away from the body.

**Effacé** — *(eh-fa-SAY)* *Effacé* means "shaded." In the general sense, it refers to any position where the dancer stands at a slight angle to the front, shading or blocking part of the body, while the feet appear open (not crossed) to the audience. In a more specific sense it is one of the eight basic directions of the body. The dancer stands at a 45° angle (three-quarter view) to the front. The foot which is furthest from the audience is extended directly in front of the body, either on the ground or in the air. The arm opposite the lifted leg is raised over the head, the other arm extended to the side in a *demi-seconde* position, or with the hand just below waist level. The upper body arches back from underneath the shoulder blades and the head is inclined to the raised arm and looking out into the audience. (see *Positions.*)

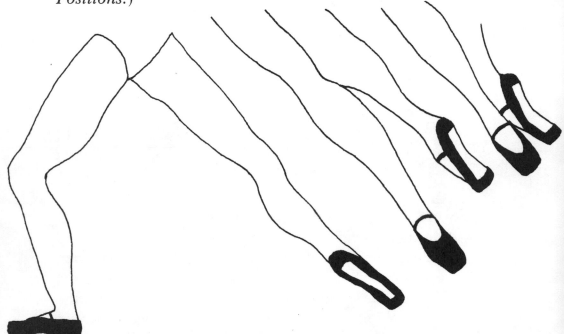

**Elévation** — *(ay-lay-va-SYAWN) Elévation* means "elevation," the ability of the dancer to jump high into the air. It is used to describe the height reached in all jumping steps *(grand jeté, cabriole,* etc.) When combined with *ballon* (which is the ability to jump and rebound off the floor like a bouncing rubber ball), the dancer can produce graceful, silky, soaring leaps. In all steps of *élévation,* the feet must be pointed the instant they leave the floor. The body must be calm and composed in the air. The landing must look soft and controlled, moving through all parts of the feet: the toes, the ball of the foot and the heel. *Elévation* is determined by how high the torso is lifted into the air, and all *élévation* steps begin and end with a *demi-plié.* Baryshnikov and Nureyev are present examples of wonderful *élévation.*

**Emboîté** — *(ahn-bwah-TAY) Emboîté* means "fitted together" or "boxed." It begins in fifth position *demi-plié*, with the right foot in back. The dancer jumps into the air and brings the right foot front with a slightly bent knee. He or she then lands in a *demi-plié* on the left leg, the right foot ending in front of the left ankle. Without stopping, the step is repeated to the other side, this time jumping onto the right leg, the left foot ending in front of the right ankle. *Emboîtés* may start from the other direction with the left leg in back. They may also be done turning and are then called "*emboîté en tournant.*" The movement remains the same except that the body does a complete turn in the air on every second jump. *Emboîté* derives its name from the fact that the feet seem "fitted together" during the movement.

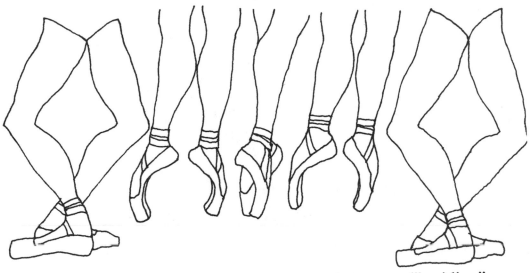

**Entrechat** — *(ahn-trih-SHAH) Entrechat* means "braiding" or "interweaving." It is any beaten step in which the dancer jumping into the air, rapidly crosses the legs in front and in back of the other before landing. *Entrechats* are followed by a number (usually from three to ten) which shows the number of crosses made by each leg. (each crossing is counted as two movements). Thus, in *entrechat quatre* (or four movements), the legs cross twice. In *entrechat six,* a most important step for the male dancer, the legs cross three times (or six movements). The even numbered *entrechats* land on two feet, the odd on one. The feet in all *entrechats* must cross from one fifth position to another. The legs move in the shape of a narrow 'V,' and do not "paddle" from side to side. It is said that the great Nijinsky could do an *entrechat dix* (ten movements) crossing the legs five times in the air before landing.

**Enveloppé** — *(ahn-vlaw-PAY) Enveloppé* literally means "enveloped." The dancer stands on one leg with the other leg fully extended. The foot of the extended leg is brought to the knee of the other leg before the foot returns to the ground in either first or fifth position.

**Epaulé** — *(ah-poh-LAY) Epaulé* means "shouldered." It is one of the eight directions of the body. The dancer stands at a 45° angle to the front (three-quarter view). The leg closest to the audience is extended directly behind the body in *arabesque.* The same arm as raised leg is extended to the front, in line with the bridge of the nose, the other arm extended back. The shoulders are square to the direction of the body and the head is inclined and turned toward the audience. (see *Positions.*)

**Epaulement** — *(ay-pohl-MAHN) Epaulement* means "shoulder movement." It describes the use of the head and the shoulders in certain positions and movements. Proper *épaulement*, or correct placing of the head and shoulders, gives ballet movement a finished and polished appearance.

**Extension** — The ability of the dancer to lift and sustain a positioned leg in the air. A dancer with good extension is able to raise and hold a leg to the side with the foot above the level of the shoulders. Women generally have better extensions than men because their bodies, particularly their hips, are far more flexible.

**Face, En** — *(ahn-FAHSS)* *En face* means "in front," or "full face." It describes any movement done facing the audience.

**Failli** — *(fa-YEE)* *Failli* means to "give away." It is a quick movement, usually done as a preparation for larger movements. The dancer stands with the legs together in fifth position, the left foot in back. Springing into the air, the body turns, the left leg opens to the back, and the left shoulder comes front, the head looking over the shoulder at the audience. The dancer lands on the right leg with the knee bent in *demi-plié* and slides the left foot along the floor from the back, through first (heels touching) to fourth, a position where the legs are about a foot apart. The left foot ends directly in front of the body. *Failli* may be done to the other side, with the right foot starting in back.

**Feet, Care of** — The dancer who spends much of the dancing day standing on her toes in hard shoes, may develop a variety of different ailments, including bunions, swollen feet and bruised or blistered toes. Other than keeping the feet clean, the toe nails short and sometimes taping the toes for protection, it is generally "grin and bear it."

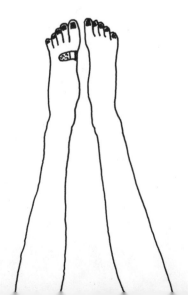

**Finger Turns** — This is a most popular turning action, done by the female dancer and her partner. The man stands behind the woman. He extends his left arm to the side and his right arm over her head, the index or third finger pointing downward. The woman takes his finger with her right hand and rests her left hand on his. She springs to *pointe*. Standing at a slight angle to the audience, she extends her right leg front. From there, she pushes off his left hand and whips the right leg first to the side, then to *passé*, closing the foot sharply to the front of the left knee. She can do many turns in this position, using the man's index finger for balance. To stop, she merely clasps the finger tightly. Finger turns may also be done to the other side, with the opposite hand and legs used.

**Fish Dive** — The *fish dive* is so named because the female dancer assumes the pose similar to that of a diving fish while being held in the air by her male partner. She may be lifted into this pose from a stationary position. She may jump into it or fall into it from a sitting position atop his shoulder.

**Floor Pattern** — Sitting high atop the balcony, it is sometimes interesting to watch the designs and patterns made by the dancers as they move across the floor. These designs and patterns are called the *floor pattern* of the dance. Throughout history, the importance of floor pattern has varied greatly. Four hundred years ago, it was the primary concern of the choreographer: the steps were limited, the costumes bulky and the audience was seated high above the dancers. If he was to capture the attention of the audience, interesting patterns of movement had to be created. However, with the appearance of the raised stage and other modern developments, floor pattern was still an important part of the dance, but no longer its *main* feature. With his wonderfully complex and beautiful floor patterns, George Balanchine has brought it into the spotlight again.

**Fokine, Michel** — *(mih-SHEL FOH-keen)* Michel Fokine was born in St. Petersburg, Russia in April of 1880. At nine he was accepted into the famous Imperial School of Ballet where he trained until his graduation in 1898. Soon after, he left to travel around the world, eventually settling in New

York in 1923, where he died in 1942.

Fokine's greatest contribution to dance was as a choreographer. In 1914, he set forth five main principles of choreography which helped to bring in the modern ballet era: 1.) Fokine believed that all steps and movements should match the subject matter and period of the work; 2.) Ballet should be faithful to the character of the music; 3.) In mime, not only the hands but the whole body should be the instrument of expression; 4.) The *Corps de ballet* should be a vital part of the dance and not just a beautiful ornament; 5.) In a ballet, the dancing should be as important as the music and decor. Among his most famous works are: *The Firebird, Les Sylphides, Petrouchka* and *La Spectre de la Rose.*

**Fondu, Fondue** — *(fawn-DEW) Fondu* means "to melt." It describes any smooth, controlled lowering of the body by the bending of one leg. Saint Leon wrote, *"Fondu* is on one leg what *demi-plié* is on two."

**Fonteyn, Margot** — One of the world's best loved ballerinas and one who continued to dance well past her fifties, Margot Fonteyn was born Peggy Hookhan in 1919. In her childhood she studied in Shanghai, China, but soon moved to England where she made her debut as a Snowflake in the *Nutcracker* with the Sadler's Wells (now Royal) Ballet in 1934. She quickly rose to become the company's greatest star, dancing in all the classics: *Giselle, Swan Lake, Sleeping Beauty, Romeo and Juliet.* She danced in many of the ballets of choreographer Frederick Ashton, including *Les Patineurs, Cinderella,* and one of her most famous roles, as the lead in *Ondine.* She was slowly moving toward retirement in the early 1960s when she met Rudolf Nureyev, whose youth and energy revived her dancing. Together they became one of the most famous ballet partnerships the world has ever known. Margot Fonteyn was blessed with a beautiful face and body, a refined technique and was one of the greatest lyric and dramatic ballerinas of our time. Dame Margot once toured the world extensively, dancing with many partners and appeared in several movies. Today, she is the President of the Royal Academy of Dancing, school of the Royal Ballet.

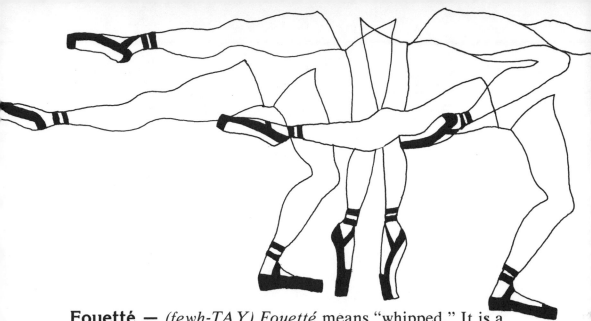

**Fouetté** — *(fewh-TAY) Fouetté* means "whipped." It is a general terms which includes any whipping action of the body, either by the extended leg whipping from one position to another or the upper body from one direction to another. While there are many different kinds of *fouetté,* it is the *grand fouettés en tournant* (usually just called *fouettés*) which we shall now describe. These *fouettés* are a series of turns done on one leg. The ballerina is propelled by the other leg whipping in and out from an extended position. *Fouettés* are done on *pointe* and in one spot. The technical details are as follows: *fouettés* usually follow a *pirouette* or another action which generates the proper force for the turn. Sinking into *demi-plié* on the *first* leg from the *pirouette*, the ballerina extends the second leg to the front. She rises to *pointe*, at the same time sweeping the second leg to the side. She does a complete turn of the body, bringing the foot of the second leg to the knee of the *first* as she does so. After the turn is completed she sinks onto the *first* leg and repeats. These *fouettés* are done *en de hors* (outward, away from the supporting leg). The thirty-two consecutive *fouettés* done in Act II of *Swan Lake* represent the most difficult technical feat for the female dancer.

**Giselle —** *Giselle* is one of the most popular and best loved ballets of all time. It is considered the crowning achievement of the Romantic Era. It is often referred to as the "Hamlet of Ballets," not only for its enduring popularity but because it offers one of the most challenging and sought after roles in dance: as *Hamlet* is to an actor, so *Giselle* is to the ballerina.

*Giselle* was first produced in 1842, choreographed by Jean Corelli and Jules Perrot, with music by Adolphe Adam. The story was based upon an old folk legend set down by the German poet, Heinrich Heine, and written for the ballet by Théophile Gautier. The choreography has changed much since its first showing in 1841. Unfortunately, since there was no system to accurately record dance at that time, what remains of the original choreography is unknown. While *Giselle* changes with each new company and each new ballerina, it remains a most noble and beautiful work.

Giselle, an innocent peasant girl, falls in love with Count Albrecht, a nobleman who lives in her village dis-

guised as a peasant named Loys. Hilarion, the local game-keeper, who is in love with Giselle and terribly jealous, tries to warn her that Albrecht is of noble blood and can never marry her. Giselle, blinded by her love for Albrecht, pays Hilarion no attention. Into the village walks the Duke of Courtland (Albrecht's uncle) and his daughter, Bathilde (Albrecht's fiancee), to rest from a hunting trip. Giselle and her mother come out to greet the newcomers and are soon joined by the villagers who have just returned from an outing with Albrecht. Much dancing and merriment follows, with several ensemble dances and a beautiful solo by Giselle.

The merriment comes to an abrupt end, however. Hilarion has found Albrecht's sword with the family name upon it (as proof of his noble background), and displays it before Hilbrecht and all the villagers. A brief fight follows and the sword is dropped to the ground. Hilarion, to further prove his point, summons the Duke and Bathilde to come forth. Giselle, still unconvinced of Albrecht's other life, rushes over to Bathilde, only to see Albrecht's engagement ring on her finger. Giselle realizes at last that she has been deceived.

Her reaction is dramatic. A sensitive and fragile girl, she is completely overcome by what has happened and begins to dance madly about the stage. Realizing that all is lost, she picks up Albrecht's sword and stabs herself. After even more dancing, Giselle dies in her mother's arms.

In the second act, the scene shits to a forest glade. There the grieving Albrecht prays before Giselle's tomb. It appears, however, that Hilarion has preceded him and has been captured by Queen Myrtha and her band of Wilis — girls who, like Giselle, died before their wedding day. Hilarion was thrown into a lake to drown. Myrtha has a similar plan for Albrecht, but Giselle, who loves him still, tries to save him. She tells him to seek safety by the cross above her tomb. Angrily, Myrtha decrees that he must dance with Giselle until death, instead. They dance a beautiful, unearthly *pas de deux* together, followed by two difficult solos, and more dancing. Giselle pleads with the Wilis to let them stop, but to no avail. Finally, his strength gone, Albrecht falls exhausted to the ground.

The hour of dawn is approaching, and the Wilis must return to their graves. Giselle holds the fallen Albrecht in her arms for a last moment, then returns to her own tomb. As she does, Albrecht desperately reaches out to try to bring her back, but cannot, and falls back to the ground.

**Glissade** — *(glee-SOD) Glissade* means "to glide." The feet glide along the floor, one after the other. A *glissade* is used as a preparation step or as a link from one step to another. The dancer stands in a *demi-plié* in fifth position. One foot (called the "working foot") brushes along the floor until the toe rises, fully pointed, several inches off the floor. Next he or she pushes off the other foot (called "the supporting foot"), straightening the knee and pointing the toe so that both legs are fully extended in the air for one moment. The weight is then transferred to the working leg and the knee bends. This leaves the supporting leg extended a few inches off the floor. The supporting leg then closes along the floor into a fifth position. *Glissades* may be done to the front, back or side and with or without changing the front-back relationship of the feet.

**Grand Battement** — *(gran bat-MAHN) Grand battement* means "a large beat." As an exercise done at the *barre*, it is used to increase the mobility of the hip sockets. On the floor it is used as a preparation for jumping actions. Standing with the legs together in first or fifth position, the dancer kicks one leg into the air as quickly and as freely as possible, then brings it down slowly and with great control. The extended or "working foot" must brush along the floor before going to and returning from the *grand battement*. It must be fully pointed the stant it leaves the floor. The working leg must remain straight throughout the exercise. When *grand battements* are done to the front and side, the hips and upper body remain straight and still. When done to the back, the upper body moves slightly forward to balance the lifting of the leg.

**Grand Fouetté** — *(grahn fewh-TAY)* This step, which means "a large whipping action," is one of several major leaping actions found in ballet. It involves any rapid turning of the upper body toward or away from the extended leg while in the air. The technique is as follows: springing into the air, the dancer sweeps one leg to the front, whips the upper body away from the extended leg, then lands in *demi-plié* with the extended leg directly behind the body in *arabesque. Grand fouetté* may also be done in the opposite direction, the leg first extending back and ending front, or to the side and ending either front or back.

**Grand Jeté** — *(grahn zheh-TAY) Grand jeté* mean "a large throw," and is one of the most beautiful of all major leaping actions. It is often used by photographers in action shots of dancers. Beginning with a *préparation* step (or "running start"), the dancer rises swiftly from the floor, stretching one leg to the front, the other to the back in a split or near-splie position. The body then makes a large arc in the air before lightly landing on the front leg. The back leg remains extended with the knee straight.

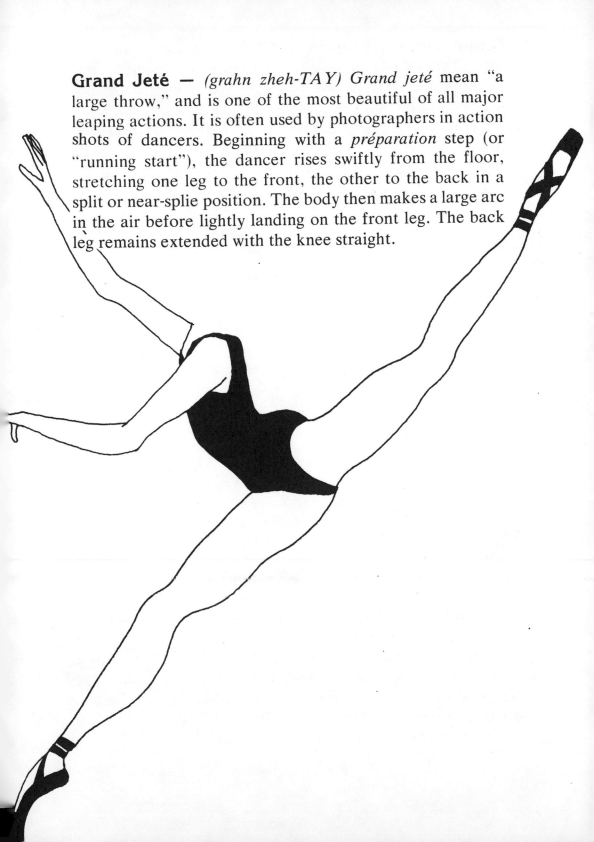

## Grand Jeté En Tourant — *(grahn zheh-TAY ahn toor-NAHn) Grand jeté en tournant,* sometimes nicknamed *"tour jeté,"* means a "large *jeté* turning," and is another of the major leaping actions. Taking a *préparation* step, or "running start," the dancer bounds into the air, throwing the first leg to the front, and bringing the second leg to meet it. The body then turns around in the air. The second leg sweeps by the first and the dancer lands on the first leg in *demi-plié.* The second leg is extended in back or *arabesque.*

## Grand Pas De Basque — *(grahn pah duh BOSK) Grand pas de basque* means "a large *pas de basque."* The dancer sweeps the *first* leg from the front to the side, followed by a sweep of the second leg from the side to the front. The second leg crosses over the *first* leg while still in the air. Upon landing, the dancer steps forward on the second leg, closing the *first* leg in fifth position back.

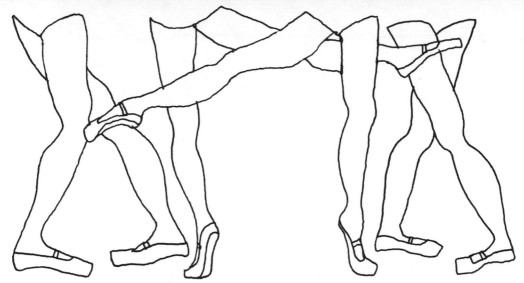

**Grand Pirouette** — *(grahn peer-oo-WET) Grand pirouette* means "a large *pirouette.*" It is a series of turning actions done primarily by the male dancer. It can be done in two ways, either separately or combined. 1.)Standing in one spot, the *danseur* does a series of quick little hops on one leg in *demi-plié,* rapidly turning the body with the other leg extended to the side. 2.) The danseur executes one, two or many turns with the leg again extended to the side. This time, however, he rises to *demi-pointe* (lifting the heel of the other leg) with each turn or turns. To finish, he brings the foot of the extended leg to the knee of the other, does many turns in this position, and closes. (see *Pirouette.*)

# H

**Haut, En** — *(ah-NOH) En haut* means "on high." It refers to a position where the arms are raised over the head, assuming the shape of an oval. The palms face the floor, the finger tips about an inch apart. The arms in an *en haut* position are said to "frame" the head.

# I

**Injuries** — As with anyone engaged in sport or hard physical activity, dancers, too, suffer from a variety of injuries. Most common are pulled muscles or tendons, sprained ankles, twisted knees, even broken bones. These injuries, which can hamper or even ruin a career, may stem from fatigue, overwork or accidents, but most frequently are a result of improper training.

The process of training the body to perform ballet is a long and delicate one. Every position is unnatural to the body and the muscles must learn each one slowly. It has been said that it takes ten years to make a dancer. Unfortunately, many unqualified teachers will try to "hurry things along," and seriously injure their students in the process. Students are forced to rotate or turn out their legs before they are ready. This may cause damage to the knees, ankles and backs. Young girls are often allowed to put on point shoes before their bones and muscles can support them, sometimes permanently ruining their feet and backs.

Since ballet is an art which must be practiced every day, a certain amount of injury will happen. But with proper training and sound working habits, most can be avoided.

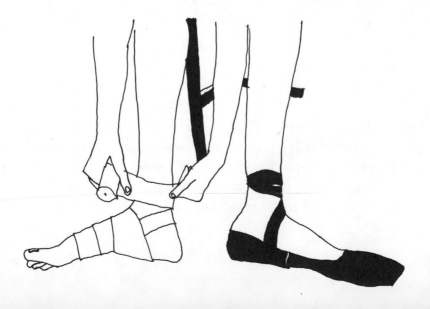

# J

**Jeté** — *(zheh-TAY) Jeté* means "thrown." It is used to describe any jump from one foot to another in which the leg seems to be thrown. In general, it refers to a particular step which may be described as follows: Standing with the legs together in fifth position, the dancer brushes the *first* leg off the floor. At the same time he or she uses the second leg to spring into the air. While in the air, the heel of the second leg is quickly drawn to the base of the calf of the *first*. The dancer lands in this position in *demi-plié. Jetés* may be done to the front, side or back or with a beat.

**The Joffrey Ballet** — The Joffrey Ballet was founded by dancer, teacher, choreographer Robert Joffrey in May of 1954. It began with one station wagon, four ballets, six dancers and one tape recorder, but quickly grew. By 1960 it was touring the country in full force and with a complete orchestra.

In 1962, Rebeccah Harkness, a wealthy patroness of the arts, decided to support the financially troubled company. Within a year the repertoire was expanded and the company was asked to tour the Soviet Union. Not long afterwards, Robert Joffrey decided to break from Ms. Harkness, and the company was forced to disband.

Then, in 1964, with the help of a Ford Foundation Grant, the Joffrey Company was reborn, and thrives to this day. It performs at New York City Center and tours the country. It has a company school called "American Ballet Center" in Greenwich Village. It is a young company, composed mostly of dancers in their early or mid-twenties. While they may lack the experience of older dancers, the Joffrey members more than make up for it with their great spirit and energy. The company rarely performs the classics.

73

Instead, it performs all types of dance: jazz, modern and ballet. While Gerald Arpino is now principal choreographer for the company, the works of many choreographers have been used including those by Frederick Ashton, Agnes De Mille, John Cranko and Leonide Massine. The company has no "star" system, and offers a most refreshing and vital look into American dance today.

**Jumps** — See *Elévation.*

# K

**Kirkland, Gelsey** — At the tender age of twenty-six, Gelsey Kirkland has emerged as one of the most exciting young ballerinas of the Western World. Born in Bucks County, Pennsylvania, in December of 1952, she moved to Manhattan at age three, where her playwright father, Jack Kirkland, decided she should prepare for a life in the theater. Several years later she was accepted into the School of American Ballet (New York City Ballet's training ground) and immediately threw herself, heart and soul, into dancing. She was asked to join the company at fifteen and soon became a favorite of artistic director, George Balanchine. He gave her the "run of the repertoire," including the leading roles in *Jewels, Symphone in C, Harlequinade* and others.

But it was not enough. Wanting to dance the classics and expand her repertoire, Gelsey began to feel hemmed in at New York City Ballet and was ready for a change. Luckily, a young Russian dancer was soon to provide her with the chance.

His name was Baryshnikov, and in 1974 he defected from the Kirov Company and soon came to the United States. Looking for a partner, he felt that Gelsey's small size would be an ideal match for his 5'-6'' frame, and requested that she come to American Ballet Theater and dance with him.

It was magic from the start. The two performed together in *Les Sylphides, La Fille Mal Gardeé* and others. Their *Giselle* in 1975 was hailed as a triumph. Gelsey seemed on top of the dance world and set for a long and glorious career.

But her sudden fame may have proved too much for her and her career began to go sour. She became impossible to work with and her weight dropped to eighty pounds. She was supposed to appear in the movie, The Turning Point, but ill health forced her to bow out. Her whole career seemed in jeopardy.

Fortunately, she was able to snap out of it and has made a remarkable comeback. Her stamina and spirits have returned. She has begun to relax and enjoy life a bit more. In the fall of 1977, she was asked to play the leading role of Carla in Baryshnikov's *Nutcracker* which appeared on national television. Now firmly rooted in American Ballet Theater and on the track once again, her famous "legs of steel" and wonderfully fluid style should enchant audiences for years to come.

# L

**Leotard** — Elastic, one-piece garment worn for class and on stage.

**Louis XIV** — Louis XIV, known as the "Sun King," was born in 1638. He became King of France in 1643 and reigned until 1715. Very interested in the dance, he improved the quality of the court ballets and even appeared in them himself. In 1661, he established the Royal Academy of Music and Dance, the first school designed solely for the training of dancers.

# M

**McBride, Patricia** — Patricia McBride is an American born and trained ballerina. A principal dancer with the New York City Ballet, she was a frequent partner of Edward Villella. She studied at the School of American Ballet, began her dance career with the Andre Eglevsky Ballet Company and joined New York City Ballet in 1959. She has appeared in such major roles as Sugar Plum fairy in *Nutcracker,* Columbine in *Harlequinade,* Hermia in *A Midsummer Night's Dream,* as well as in many *pas de deux* with Edward Villella. (see *Villella.*)

**Makarova, Natalia** — At thirty-nine, Makarova is one of the world's greatest ballerinas. She was born in Leningrad, Russia in 1940, where she attended the Leningrad Ballet School and graduated in 1959. She defected from the Soviet Union in 1970 and has since spent most of her time dancing with the American Ballet Theater. At home in both the classics and more modern works, her fiery presence and wonderful acting make her a favorite of audiences everywhere. She has danced with many great male dancers and recently appeared on public television with Baryshnikov in *Giselle*.

**Manège, En** — *(Ahn mah-NEZH) En manège* means "roundabout." When the dancer travels in a circle around the room or stage while performing a combination of steps or turns, this is *en manége*.

**Methods of Teaching** — While there are perhaps five basic methods or "schools of thought" for the teaching of ballet, two are most often used in this country. One is called the *"Italian"* or *"Cecchetti School."* The other is loosely called the *"Russian School."* Some teachers are strict followers of one school. Other teachers combine certain elements of the two into their own system. Both schools aim to teach their students how to dance. It is their approach to teaching which differs.

The *Cecchetti* method (developed by a man of the same name over a hundred years ago) is a strict approach to the learning of ballet technique. It uses a series of specific exercises and movements, which, while they are not really dancing, do give the student certain principles of body control. These principles may later be applied to all ballet movements and steps.

The *Russian School* is a far looser approach. The exercises are much the same, but are usually longer and more complicated. This allows the student greater freedom to move and dance across the floor. It is hoped that he or she will learn the principles of dancing by doing and repeating.

The critics of the *Cecchetti* system claim that it produces very correct, but "stiff" dancers. Those opposed to the *Russian* system believe its students may move with greater ease, but are generally sloppy.

**Mime** — Ballet is a language which tells a story and expresses emotion by means of certain steps and gestures. The language of steps is called "technique." The language of gesture is called "mime." There are over a hundred standard gestures in the ballet. A century ago these gestures could directly relate the story of a ballet to the audience. Today, however, most mime sections have been cut out and

the story is told in the program. There are several gestures
which still remain. Circling of the hands over the head
means "dance." One hand pressed to the heart, the other
pointing to the ceiling with the index and third fingers
extended means "love." The fists crossed and lowered in
front of the body means "death." Shaking the fists above the
head means "anger." And so forth.

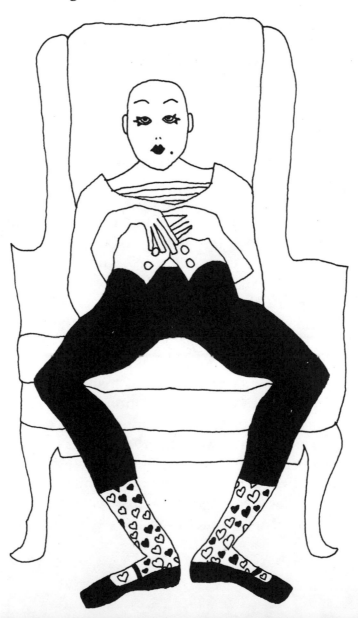

**New York City Ballet** — New York City Ballet was founded in 1948 by Lincoln Kirstein. It is unique among the major companies of the world because it exists mainly to serve the philosophy and ideas of one man, twentieth century's foremost choreographer, George Balanchine. Over the past thirty years, "Balanchine and Company," (with considerable help from co-choreographer, Jerome Robbins) has evolved a look and style of ballet which has revolutionized the art and whose influence is felt world-wide.

To better understand the company, it is necessary to talk first about the dancers. Since it is Balanchine's belief that "ballet is women," women play the lead role in the company (although on the strength of his work, Balanchine has attracted many of the world's finest dancers — both male and female — to come and work for him). Generally speaking, these dancers conform to what is called the "Balanchine body," that is, tall and thin, with unusually long legs, small heads and great flexibility. They are trained to perform *his* style of choreography and Balanchine does not tolerate dancers who wish to dance for their own personal glory. He wants only those willing to be "messengers" of his works. The list of those who are willing is certainly an impressive one: Suzanne Farrell, Peter Martins, Patricia McBride, Sara Leland, Kay Mazzo, Allegra Kent, Edward Villella, and now Mikhail Baryshnikov, to name a few.

Now, a look at his style. Balanchine's works are lean, fast and cold. They demand that the dancer perform complex movements and patterns, many times on a bare stage, without much feeling or emotion. "Ballet should speak for itself," Balanchine says. It needs no fancy decor or story to bring pleasure to an audience. All that is needed are the pure, beautiful movements and lines of well-trained dancers on stage. Frequently he uses the music of modern composers, most often Igor Stravinsky.

Because of its distinct look and style, New York City

Ballet does not enjoy universal appeal. Indeed, it has often been criticized for its lack of variety and warmth as well as its often difficult-to-understand ballets. But this cricitism misses the point. The company was not founded to show a balanced repertoire or the standard ballets of the past, but new and unusual dance of the present. For the past thirty years, it has done just that. New York City Ballet performs at the New York State Theater in Lincoln Center for most of the year, spending a few weeks each summer at Saratoga, in upstate New York. (see *Balanchine* and *Stravinsky.)*

**Nijinsky, Vaslav** — *(ni-ZHEEN-ski)* Vaslav Nijinsky was born in 1890 in Kiev, Russia. His parents were both professional dancers. He was accepted into the Imperial Ballet School at age ten and soon became one of its most outstanding pupils, graduating in 1908. After he began with the Imperial Ballet, Nijinsky met Serge Diaghilev, a man who was to shape his entire ballet career. Diaghilev was about to form a new company called the *Ballets Russes* (Ballet Russian), and asked Nijinsky to be his *premier danseur.*

81

Nijinsky appeared with the company in their Paris debut in May of 1909. He was an overnight sensation. With the exception of a brief return to the Imperial Ballet, Nijinsky remained with the Ballets Russes for five years. He danced many leading roles including two of his most famous, *La Spectre de la Rose* and *Petrouchka,* both by choreographer Michel Fokine. In addition, Nijinsky tried choreographing. His own works broke away from the elegant and fluid movements of ballet and used angular and jerky movements of his own invention. Unfortunately, Europe was not ready for his ideas, and only his *Afternoon of the Fawn* met with any kind of success.

Then in 1913, misfortune struck. Diaghilev remained behind in Europe while the Ballets Russes went on a South American tour. In Buenos Aires, Nijinsky decided to marry fellow dancer Romola Pulszky without asking Diaghilev's permission. Diaghilev, a possessive man who had a close relationship with Nijinsky, was furious when he heard the news and had Nijinsky immediately dismissed from the company. Unable to cope with the dismissal, the career of this sensitive young dancer began to slowly decline.

The next year Nijinsky tried to form his own company, but it failed to get off the ground when he became ill. When World War I began, he was held prisoner in Austria (his wife's country) for two years. Finally he was allowed to rejoin the Ballets Russes on a tour of the United States in 1916; later he organized a tour for yet another of his companies, but both tours were unsuccessful. Several years later, his career in ruins, Nijinsky went tragically insane and remained so until his death in 1950.

Over the past couple of decades much has been written about this strange man's life, and Nijinsky does present the historian with many interesting problems. His career only lasted some nine years and he left no movies and few photographs of his dancing for us to see. While no one will deny that he was the greatest male dancer of his time, a tremendous jumper, several male dancers of today (including Baryshnikov and Nureyev) can duplicate his technical feats and certainly show greater endurance and consistency than he did. One is tempted to ask: Does he merit so much attention? Just how good a dancer was he?

Actually, neither question is a fair one, for a dancer's ability cannot be determined only by how high he jumps or how many times he performs. Much more is involved. There is stage presence, and that magical ability of great dancers to capture the character they are portraying and bring it to life. Unfortunately, such things cannot be recorded. Instead, one can only listen to the glowing reports from those who saw him, look at the pictures and imagine. (see *Diaghilev, Serge.*)

**Noverre, Jean George** — *(zhahn zhorzh no-VAHR)* Jean George Noverre was a famous French choreographer and dancer who was born near Paris in 1727. He studied with the well known French dancer, Louis Dupré, and made his debut in Paris in 1743. Noverre made several contributions to dance, most of which were set forth in his *Lettres Sur La Danse Et Sur Les Ballets (*Notes on Dance and Ballets) written in 1760.

Noverre was the first to treat ballet as an art and not as mere entertainment. He was the creater of the *ballet d'action,* or the ballet which told a story in dance and mime. Through his efforts, the tradition of wearing masks during performances was eliminated as were certain dated gestures and movements which made up most of the ballets of his time. Unfortunately, his ideas were too advanced for Paris and he was forced to go abroad to put these ideas into use. Called the "Shakespeare of the dance," Noverre died in 1810.

**Nureyev, Rudolf** — *(neur-YAY-ev)* Rudolf Nureyev is without a doubt one of the finest dancers of his generation. Not since the great Nijinsky a half century before has any male dancer enjoyed Nureyev's enormous success. He has done a great deal to boost ballet's popularity.

Nureyev was born in 1938 in the province of Ufa, Russia, where as a child he endured hunger and poverty with his poor family. His early ballet training was irregular. He studied privately with a local teacher and danced with a local folk group. At sixteen, he was able to save the necessary funds to go to Leningrad and was accepted into the highly respected Leningrad School of Ballet (once called The Imperial School.) He received a lot of "put-downs" by students and teachers alike for his advanced age, his "country" ways and lack of training. But he was not to be stopped. By sheer will and determination he soon made up for lost time and was allowed to study with the great teacher Pushkin, who had taught Nijinsky. Within just three years, Nureyev was promoted to soloist in the Kirov company, dancing in many of the company's leading roles.

While the Kirov was beginning a Paris-London-New York tour in 1961, Nureyev made his famous "leap" to freedom. A highly individual man, he was upset with the strict rules and attitude of the company. He wanted greater artistic and personal freedom. Nureyev had been at odds with the management for some time and a break was near at hand. As the company was boarding the plane to London, Nureyev defected by running away and leaping into the arms of the French police. He became an overnight sensation. Soon he made his way to London where he joined the Royal Ballet as a guest artist and began his famous partnership with Margot Fonteyn.

Nureyev has since appeared with almost every major ballet company outside the Soviet Union, dancing both modern and classical roles, has performed on television and made several movies.

Nureyev is one of dance's most controversial and disorderly characters. Well known are his bad temper and often embarrassing antics off-stage. But he is a *brilliant* dancer, gifted with a certain animal magnetism and the ability to give everything he has for every performance. He has brought increased respect to the male dancer. His willingness to dance with lesser known companies has given them the recognition they so sorely need. With advancing age — he is now forty-one — Nureyev pushes himself on, dancing night after night, although he now prefers to dance less ballet and perform more modern works. (see *Fonteyn.)*

**The Nutcracker —** *The Nutcracker* is probably the best known and most frequently staged ballet. At Christmas time throughout the world, companies large and small bring their own version of *Nutcracker* to the stage. The delightful music and fanciful story appeal to audiences of all ages. It was first produced in St. Petersburg (now Leningrad) in 1892, with choreography by Lev Ivanov and Marius Petipa, music by Peter Tchaikovsky. It is based on a story by E.T.A Hoffman called *The Nutcracker and the King of Mice.* While, as has been said, the versions vary from company to company, the basic story goes something like this:

One Christmas Eve a little girl named Clara, whose parents are having a party, receives a gift of a Nutcracker from a strange gentleman named Drosselmeyer. Later that night, she falls asleep and dreams of a battle between the toy soldiers (which were also a gift) and some mice. The Nutcracker tries boldly to fight the King of the Mice but must be saved by Clara, who throws her shoe at the King. The Nutcracker is then transformed into a handsome prince who takes Clara on a voyage through the land of the snowflakes to Konfitürenberg, the home of the Sugar Plum Fairy. There everyone dances before Clara and the prince in their honor. (see *Petipa* and *Tchaikovsky.)*

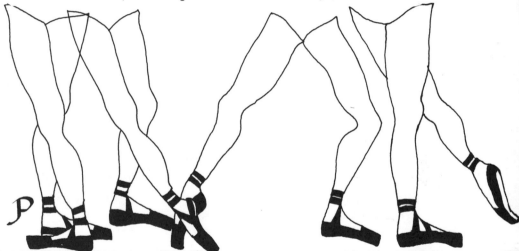

**Pas De Basque —** *(pah duh BAHSK) Pas de basque* means "a step of the Basque." It is a step taken from the dances of the Basque people of Northern Spain and Southwestern France. Standing in fifth position with the right foot in front, the dancer brushes the right foot along the floor in a semi-circle to the side. Then jumping onto that leg in *demi-plié*, he or she leaves the left leg extended. In one sweeping movement, the left leg closes into first, then fifth position and with the knee bent, slides to the front. The weight is taken onto the left leg, leaving the right leg free to close behind into fifth position. *Pas de basque* may also be done to the other side, the left foot starting front. (A version of this step is used by Dorothy and her friends as they march down the "yellow-brick road" in *The Wizard Of Oz.)*

**Pas De Bourrée —** *(pah duh boo-RAY) Pas de bourrée* means a *"bourrée* step." The *bourrée* is the native dance of Auvergne, in south central France. It is used to connect one movement with another. *Pas de bourrée* is done in many ways, to the front, back, side or turning. However it is done, the mechanics of the step remain the same. To avoid confusion, the *pas de bourrée dessous* (or *pas de bourrée* "under") will be described. Standing with the legs together in fifth position, the dancer brushes the *right* leg to the side, lifting the toe a few inches off the floor. The *right* leg closes sharply behind the left as the dancer rises to *demi-pointes.* While on *demi-pointe,* the left leg opens to the side, the *right* foot is brought in front of the left and the heels are lowered into fifth position *demi-plié.* This may be also be done to the other side with the left leg starting the movement. Women perform a slightly more complicated version of this step. When the *right* foot closes behind the left, the female dancer rises to *pointe,* bringing the left foot to the *right* knee. The left foot opens to the side on *pointe* and the *right* leg comes to the left knee. The feet come together and close in fifth position *demi-plié.*

**Pas De Bourrée Couru** — *(pah duh boo-RAY koo-REW)*
*Pas de bourrée couru* means "a *pas de bourrée* running." It is a series of quick, even steps with the feet close together done by the female dancer as she runs smoothly about the stage. *Bourrées,* as they are called, may be done either on *demi-* or full *pointe.*

**Pas De Chat** — *(pah duh SHAH) Pas de chat* means "step of the cat." Standing in fifth position, the dancer raises and bends the right leg at the knee and springing into the air, repeats the action on the left leg. At the height of the jump the toes are almost touching. The landing is made on the right leg, immediately followed by the left into fifth position *demi-plié.* The *pas de chat* may also be done to the other side, beginning with the left leg. It must also be noted that this is only one of many types of *pas de chat*, and the position of the legs in the air may vary depending on which type is used.

**Pas De Ciseaux** — *(pah duh see-ZOH) Pas de ciseaux* means "scissors step." The dancer opens and closes the legs like the blades of a scissors. Beginning and ending in fifth position, the dancer jumps into the air, splitting the legs to the side as far as possible. Many times in character roles, the male dancer will bend over and touch his toes while in the air.

**Pas De Deux** — *(pah duh DUH) Pas de deux* means "a dance for two." In classical ballet it refers to that section of the ballet, sometimes called the *grand pas de deux*, in which the ballerina and her partner dance together alone on stage. It is composed of six parts: *Entrée* or *Intrada* (the entrance), *Adagio* (the slow, graceful movement of the ballerina while supported by her partner), the male variation or solo, the female variation, and the *coda* (the rousing finish in which the male and female dancer alternate, then dance together). *Swan Lake, Giselle* and *Sleeping Beauty* all have excellent examples of *pas de deux*.

**Pas Marché** — *(pah mar-SHAY)* Pas marché means "a marching step," but is used to describe the graceful, ordered walk of the classical dancer. The right leg gradually extends forward, presenting a fully pointed and turned-out foot to the audience. This is followed by a bend or *fondu* on the left leg. The dancer then steps out onto the right foot and lowers it smoothly through all three parts of the foot: first the toes, then the ball of the foot and the heel. The step is then repeated on alternate legs.

**Passé** — *(pa-SAY)* Passé means "to pass." The foot of one leg passes by the knee of the second leg when moving from one position to another. In everyday usage, however, *passé* refers to that position where the foot of one leg attaches itself firmly to the front of the knee of the other. The lifted foot must be fully pointed and turned out, so that only the little toe touches the knee cap. The dancer's legs form a triangle (the strongest and most secure design found in nature).

**Penché** — *(pawn-SHAY) Penché* means "to tilt." The dancer further raises an already extended leg, tilting the upper body away from the leg at the same time. While *penchés* may be done in all directions, *arabesque penché* is most frequently used.

92

**Pavlova, Anna** — Anna Pavlova was born in St. Petersburg, Russia in 1881, the daughter of a peasant and a laundress. She was a frail child, but was accepted into the Imperial Ballet School despite her weakness. Soon she became an outstanding pupil. Later, she was afforded the unheard-of opportunity of dancing with the Imperial Ballet while still a student and by 1906 was dancing the company's leading roles as *prima ballerina.*

Beginning in 1907, Pavlova occasionally left Russia to tour both the United States and Europe. She danced with small groups and with Diaghilev's Ballets Russes, performing with such partners as Michel Fokine, Nicholas Legat and the great Vaslav Nijinsky. In 1913, Pavlova decided to cut her contacts with the Imperial Ballet completely, and left Russia forever.

Following her decision, she came to America where she founded her own company and spent the next sixteen years traveling and dancing around the world. She logged over half-a-million miles during this period, and danced virtually everywhere outside Russia.But her hard schedule was to take its toll. In 1931, her energy gone, Pavlova came down with pneumonia while working in a cold studio and soon died.

Pavlova was a true artist, undoubtedly the finest ballerina of the first three decades of this century. She could invest her dancing with such freshness that no matter how many times she performed a work, it was as if she were performing it for the first time. She had a lively sense of style and always danced with simplicity and beauty, making "her features speak and her body sing."

Pavlova drew from a rather undistinguished repertoire, derived mainly from such classics as *Don Quixote* and *Swan Lake*. But as far as history is concerned, her choice of repertoire hardly matters for she gave ballet something far greater. Pavlova brought it away from the royal theaters of Europe and into the small towns and cities across the world. During her incredible journey, she performed in run-down theaters, high school gyms and many times before an audience which had never seen or *heard* of ballet before. Most important, Pavlova gave herself unselfishly to her art and has given countless generations of dancers an example to follow and try to equal.

**Petipa, Marius** — Marius Petipa was born in Marseilles, France in 1819. He began his dance career in Nantes in 1838, moved to Russia nine years later and remained there until his death in 1910.

Petipa is known as the father of classical ballet, creating or restaging some sixty full-length works, many of which are still performed (with some modification) today. He was a thorough and careful choreographer. He always researched the subject matter of his work and paid close attention to stage decor and music. Petipa believed choreography was the most important aspect of the production. Among his most famous works are: *Don Quixote, La Bayadere* and *Sleeping Beauty*, as well as the restaging of *Giselle, Paquita, Le Corsaire, La Sylphide* and *Swan Lake* (Acts I and III).

**Piqué** — *(pee-KAY)* *Piqué* means "stab" or "stabbing." The dancer steps out on one leg to *demi-* or full *pointe* raising the other leg in the air to any desired position.

**Piqué Tourné** — *(pee-PAY toor-NAY)* *Piqué tourné* means "*piqué* turning." It is a series of turns usually done by the female dancer traveling across the stage or in a circle. Stepping onto *pointe* on the right leg, the dancer immediately brings the left foot to the back of the knee or calf of the right leg and does one or two turns in that position. The left leg returns to the floor in *demi-plié* and the step is repeated. Each turn is marked by a rhythmical snap of the head, called "spotting." *Piqué* turns may be done to the other side as well, stepping out onto the left leg to start.

**Pirouette** — *(peer-oo-WET)* To *pirouette* means to "spin" or "turn." The *pirouette* done in a *passé* position is one of the most frequently used turns in ballet. For clarity, the description which follows will break down the *pirouette* into several steps, all of which must really be done at the same time. From a *demi-plié* position, the dancer brings the

foot of *one* leg (*working* leg) to the knee of the other (the supporting leg), lifting the heel of the supporting leg. The body then makes one or several turns in this position. Each turn is marked with a rhythmical snap of the head, called "spotting." Men always do *pirouettes* on *demi-pointe*, women on full *pointe*. During the turn the body must be kept in perfect balance, revolving on the supporting leg without leaning to any direction. The power for the turn comes from the preparation in *demi-plié*, the rapid closing of the arms and "spotting," never from the body or shoulders. On stage, both men and women usually do at least two consecutive revolutions of the body, a double *pirouette* — while men may do five or six turns before landing. The *pirouette* may be done in an outward direction, away from the supporting leg (called *"en de hors")* or inward toward the supporting leg (called *"en de dans")*. You may land in any number of different positions, although fifth position is most frequently used. The position of the arms may vary, but they are usually brought in close to the dancer, just below the level of the chest. For beautiful *pirouettes* it is not enough to simply spin many times before the completion of the turn, the body must stop and pause momentarily before closing or moving to the next position.

**Placement** — The placement of the body is one of the most important parts of good ballet technique. A well-placed dancer is one who has learned to maintain with ease the proper alignment of all parts of the body. This means the knees must be in line with the center of the feet, the legs turned out, the hips and spine straight. The shoulders must be relaxed, the arms resting easily in their proper position, the head poised and the weight of the body over the arch of the foot. Proper placement is learned first at the *barre* and must be maintained in all steps and positions.

**Plié, demi and grand** — *(plee-AY, duh-mee, grahn)* There are two types of *pliés*: *demi* (a half bend of the knees) and *grand* (a full bend of the knees). Both are designed to loosen and soften knee joints and achilles tendon, plus develop a sense of balance.

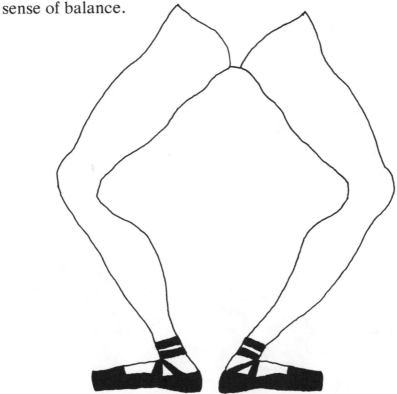

*Demi-plié:* In this movement, the knees bend as far as they can go without lifting the heels off the floor, then straighten, all in a smooth and controlled manner. The hips and back must be lifted and straight. The knees are pushed out to the side. The feet are planted firmly on the floor. When done as an exercise at the *barre,* all five positions of the feet may be used although the third position is usually omitted. Since all ballet movement begins and ends with a *demi-plié,* it is one of the most important techniques to learn.

*Grand plié:* In almost every classroom throughout the world, *grand pliés* are used as the first exercise at the *barre.* Like *demis,* they may be done in all five positions (usually omitting the third). The knees bend in the first, fourth and fifth positions, as the body is lowered until the thighs become level with the ground. As the body is lowered past the *demi-plié* position, the heels lift slightly and slowly off the floor, then return immediately as the body is raised and the knees are straightened. In second position, the heels do not come off the floor. The principles used in the *demi-plié* apply here as well: the pelvis and the back must be lifted and straight, the knees pushed out to the side and the movement smooth and controlled.

**Point Shoe or Toe Shoe** — In ballet, the point shoe is used exclusively by the female dancer. These shoes enable her to dance on the tips of her toes. They are made mostly of satin and shaped like a slipper. They have a hard open "box" at one end into which the dancer inserts her foot. On the bottom of the shoe is a wooden or metal shank which prevents the shoe from bending (and keeps the dancer from rolling over onto the front of the foot). Ribbons are tied in the shape of an "X" to the base of the leg to keep the shoe attached. Ever since their invention in the 1830s, point shoes have been a source of great "trial and tribulation" to the female dancer. When first put on they are impossibly stiff and must be "broken in." But after only a few uses they become too flexible to provide support. In fact, some dancers may go through a pair of point shoes or more in a single performance! What is worse, they are hand-made and a consistent fit is almost impossible. So much agony, for such a little shoe.

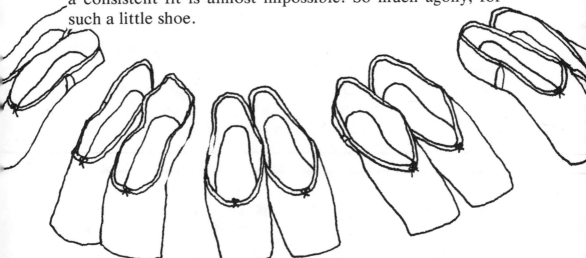

**Pointes, Sur Les** — *(sewr lay PWANT) Sur les pointes* means "on *pointe*." It is the raising of the body onto the tips of the toes, usually with the aid of a *point shoe*. Female dancers first went "on *pointe*" in the 1820s and 30s.

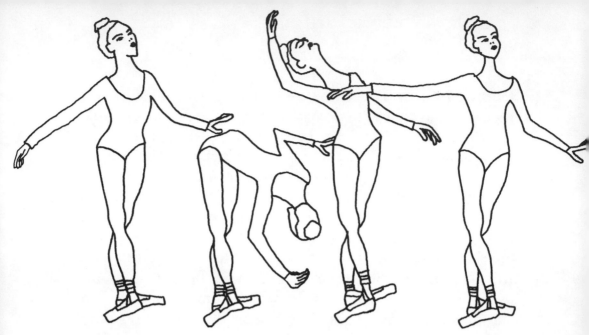

**Port De Bras** — *(pour du BRAH) Port de bras* means "carriage of the arms." The term has two meanings. One, it is used to describe the movement of the arms from one position to another. Two, it refers to a special set of exercises designed to make the arms move in a graceful, elegant manner. The importance of the arms in ballet cannot be stressed enough. The movement of the arms must seem to flow from the center of the back and the hands — never from the elbow — and the movement should be fluid and smooth. The arms are always slightly rounded. The tips of the elbows never stick out. The hands are simple and never flowery. While the legs must have a sharp, almost steely quality, the arms must appear soft and easy. It is the difference in quality and movement of the arms and the legs which produces beautiful and polished dancing. *Port de bras* is usually the last and most difficult part of technique to be acquired by the dancer.

**Posé** — *(poh-ZAY) Posé* means "poised." The dancer steps out on a straight leg onto a flat foot, *demi-pointe* or *pointe* to any desired position. When a *posé* is done to *demi-pointe* or *pointe*, it is similar to *piqué. (*see *Piqué.)*

**Position Of The Arms —** While the positions of the feet are the same in every school of ballet, the arms are not. Each method of teaching has its own arm positions. In keeping within the scope of this book, only the Cecchetti arm positions will be described:

*First position* — the arms are rounded and held at the sides with only the fingertips touching the outside of the thighs.

*Second position* — the arms are rounded and extended to the side, the elbows slightly lower than the shoulder, the wrist slightly lower than elbow. The palms face out to the audience, the hands in line with the base of the rib cage.

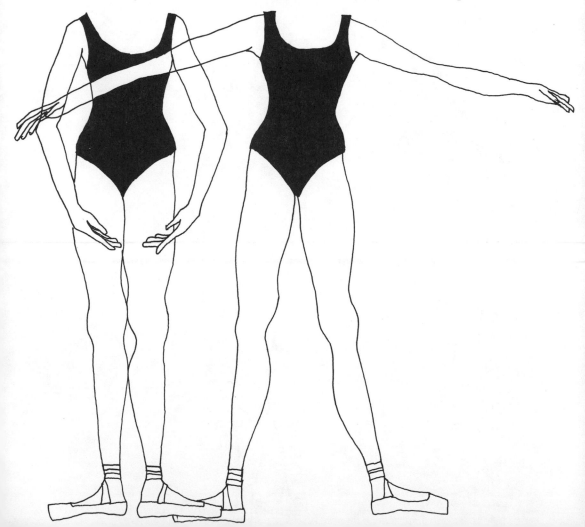

*Third position* — the arms are held with one arm curved and resting on the thigh. The other arm extends to the side in a *demi-seconde* position.

*Fourth position* — there are two fourth positions of the arms, the one *en avant* (or "in front"), the other *en haut* (or "on high"). In fourth position *en avant*, one arm is rounded in front of the body in line with the lower rib cage, while the other arm is extended to the side in second position. In fourth position *en haut*, one arm is extended to the side, the other raised over the head.

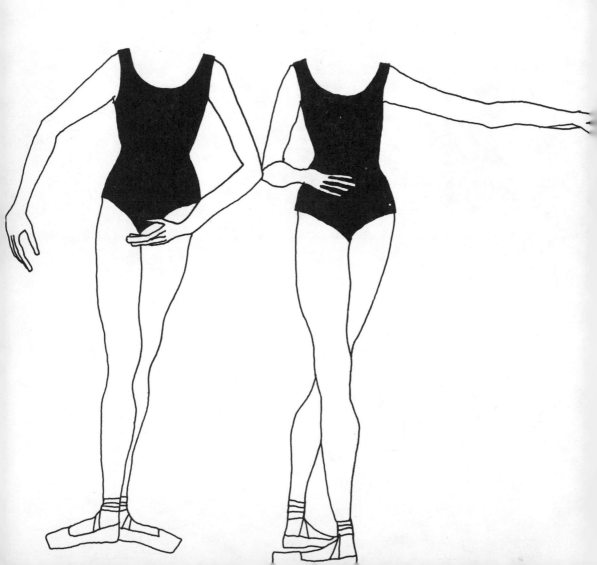

*Fifth position* — there are three fifth positions of the arms. In each one the arms are rounded as if grasping a beach ball — the fingertips a few inches apart — and form a circle. In fifth position *en bas* (or "low"), the arms are rounded, the fingertips a few inches apart, the edge of the hands touching the thighs. In fifth position *en avant* (or "front"), the arms are raised in a similar position, the palms facing the body, the hands opposite the lower rib cage. In fifth position *en haut,* the arms again form a circle, this time over and in front of the head, the finger tips remaining near the side of the head.

**Positions Of The Body** — There are eight basic positions of the body, all of which may be applied to every movement in ballet. Since each term has been described elsewhere in this book, only a brief description will follow here:

*Croisé devant* — "crossed in front." One leg appears crossed in front of the other, while the body stands at a 45° angle to the audience.

*A la quatrième devant* — "to the fourth front." One leg is extended directly front while the body faces the audience.

*Ecarté* — "thrown apart" or "separated." One leg is extended to the side while the body stands at a 45° angle to the audience.

*Effacé* — "shaded." The legs appear in an open position while the body stands at a 45° angle to the audience.

*A la seconde* — "to the second." One leg is extended to the side while the body faces the audience.

*Epaulé* — "shouldered." The leg nearest the audience is extended directly in back while the body stands at a 45° angle to the front.

*A la quatriéme derriere* — "to the fourth back." Same as *devant*, only the leg is extended back.

*Croisé derrière* — crossed in back; same as *croisé devant,* except the leg is extended back.

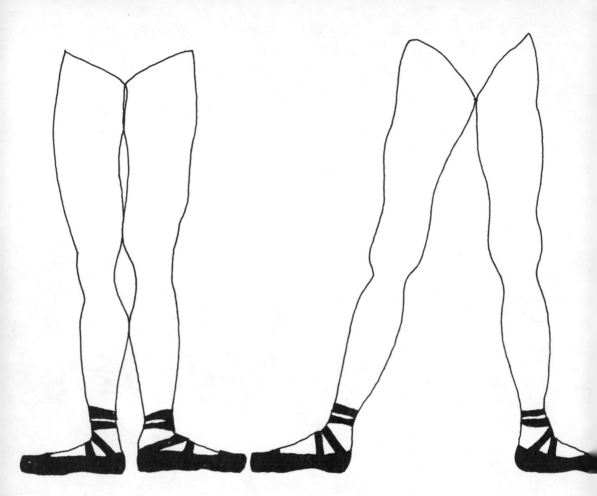

**Positions Of The Feet —** There are five basic positions of the feet, from which all ballet movement begins or ends. They were established by Pierre Beauchamps in the late 1660s.

*First Position* — the feet form a single line perpendicular (totally turned-out) to the rest of the body, the heels touching.

*Second Position* — the feet again form a single line, but the heels are separated about a foot apart.

*Third Position* — one foot is directly in front of the other, the heel of one foot touching the middle of the other. This position is rarely used.

106

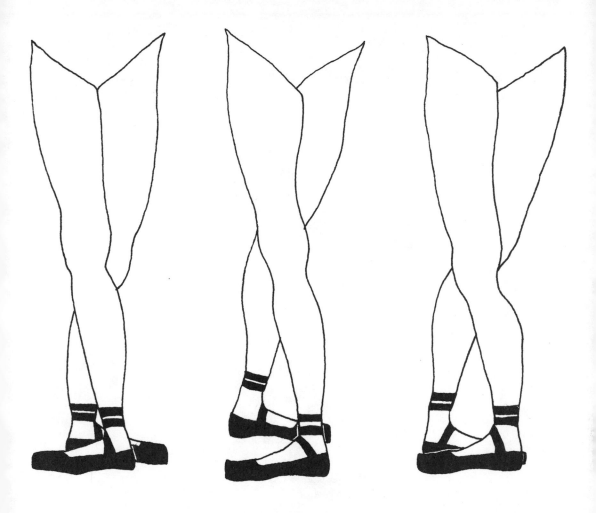

*Fourth Position* — there are two fourth positions, *open* and *closed*. In the *open* fourth position the feet are turned out, and separated by a foot or so, the heel of one foot opposite the heel of the other. In the *closed* fourth position, the feet are again separated with the heel of one foot opposite the toe of the other.

*Fifth Position* — this is the most frequently used ballet position and one which gives the body its greatest possible height. One leg is directly in front of the other, the toe of one foot touching the heel of the other, and vice versa.

107

**Positions Of The Foot** — There are four positions of the foot.

   *Quarter pointe* — the heel is raised just slightly off the floor.

   *Demi* or *half-pointe* — the heel is raised half-way between the floor and full *pointe*. In everyday usage, *demi-pointe* has become the same as three-quarter *pointe*.

   *Three quarter pointe* — the heel is raised in line with the ball of the foot.

*Sur la pointe* or *full pointe* — the female dancer stands on the tips of her toes.

**Positions Of The Head** — In the Cecchetti system, there are five basic positions of the head: 1.) Erect. 2.) Inclined to either side. 3.) Turned to one side or the other. 4.) Raised. 5.) Lowered.

**Premier Danseur** — *(pruh-MYEHR dahn-SUHR) Premier danseur* means the "first male dancer," or the highest ranking male dancer of any ballet company. People in this country are always asking what the "male ballerina" is called. The answer is the *premier danseur.*

**Préparation** — *(pray-pa-ra-SYAWN) Préparation* means "preparation." Most major steps in ballet are preceded by a *préparation*, be it a few running steps before a big jump, or a *plié* in fourth position before a *pirouette*. Generally speaking, a step is only as good as the *préparation* which comes before.

**Principal Dancer** — A principal dancer is a dancer of either sex who is the highest ranking member of any company.

**Prokofiev, Sergei** — *(pro-KOE-vee-ev)* Sergei Prokofiev was born in Russia in 1891 and died in 1953. A great composer, he provided the music for some of the best known ballets of this century. Among his most famous works are: *Romeo and Juliet, Cinderella, Peter and the Wolf, The Prodigal Son* and others.

# Q

**Quatrième derrière** — *(kah-tree-em deh-ree-AIR)* *Quatrième derrière* means "to the fourth position back." It means the foot is placed directly behind the dancer, or it means a movement must be made directly to the back. It is also one of the eight positions of the body. The dancer stands facing the audience, arms held to the side and extends one foot to the back either on the ground or raised in the air. (see *Positions.*)

**Quatrième devant** — *(ka-tree-em-duh-VAHn) Quatrième devant* means "to the fourth front." It is when the foot is to be placed directly in front or that a movement must be made directly to the front. It is also one of the eight basic positions of the body. The dancer stands facing the audience, the arms held to the side and extends one foot to the front, either on the ground or in the air. (see *Positions.)*

**Regional Ballet** — Regional ballet is used to describe all ballet activity which takes place outside New York City. Over the past two decades regional ballet has grown tremendously. Boston, Philadelphia, San Francisco, Los Angeles, Cleveland, Houston, Pittsburgh and Salt Lake can all boast of major ballet companies, with countless other cities soon to follow. The benefits of regional ballet are two-fold: 1.) It provides an opportunity for the entire country to see live ballet. 2.) It gives young and inexperienced dancers and choreographers a chance to work and perform. Many of this country's greatest dancers received their first start in regional ballet.

**Rehearsals** — The dance rehearsal has really two meanings. In one sense it is the choreographer's laboratory where he mixes and brews his ideas and dancers together to create a dance. In the other sense, it is the place where dancers must then practice what has been created over and over again until it is ready to be presented on stage. When rehearsing for a work, the first rehearsals are rather slow. The choreographer "sets" the dance, showing the dancers their various steps, and how and when they are to move on stage. This process is not a terribly long one since most dancers are able to learn and retain the choreography quickly. The following rehearsals are the most difficult. The dancers practice their parts again and again while the choreographer corrects, advises, yells, screams or does whatever is necessary to bring about his creation. Whole hours may be spent on one section and it is difficult to count the number of hours necessary to bring a dance to the stage. Most professional dancers arrive at the studio at 10:00 a.m. for morning class, rehearse all afternoon either in the studio or on the stage, then perform at night.

**Relevé** — *(reh-leh-VAY) Relevé* means "raised." With a slight spring, the dancer lifts the heels off the floor rising to either *demi* or *full pointe. Relevé* may be done in all five positions of the feet or in *arabesque, attitude, passé,* etc.

**Repertoire —** The collection of dances that a company or dancer performs.

**Révérance —** *(ray-va-RAHnS) Révérance* means "reverence" or "curtsey." It is used to describe the set of bows taken by the dancers at the end of a performance to acknowledge the applause of the audience. Unlike the curtain calls used in other types of theater, the ballet *révérance* is a long and elaborate affair, as important as the dance itself. The dancers remain in character and react to the audience with a mixture of pride and humility. After most classical ballets, roses will be brought to the leading ballerina who selects one and hands it to her partner. He takes the rose and presses it lovingly to his heart. The audience roars its approval all the while.

**Romantic Ballet —** Romantic ballet was an outgrowth of the romantic movement of the mid-nineteenth century which brought great change to all the arts. Perhaps it can be best described as an age of "soaring," when humanity broke free from the cold, almost mathematical purity of the classical age and into a world where individual expression and personal feelings became important. Artists' thoughts turned from the drab and bitter world of reality to soar into the world of dream and imagination.

Ballet was completely transformed. The woman became the dominant figure. Women began dancing on their toes and wearing long flowing skirts, giving a light, airy quality. The subject matter changed from mythological and heroic themes to fairy tales and folk legends. These stories usually dealt with two levels. There was the harsh world of reality which usually brought tragedy to the heroine and hero, and the higher world where through the power of love, the tragedy was resolved. The Age of Romantic Ballet was ushered in by its greatest ballerina, Marie Taglioni, with the production of *La Sylphide* in 1832. The most remarkable achievement of the Romantic Era came nine years later with *Giselle,* a ballet which today still serves as its greatest example.

**Rond De Jambe —** *(rawn duh ZHAMB) Rond de jambe* means "round of the leg." It is a general term used to describe any circular movement made by an extended leg either on the ground or in the air.

**Rond de jambe à terre —** *(rahn duh zhamb ah TAIR) Rond de jambe à terre* means "a *rond de jambe* on the ground." It refers to an exercise done primarily at the *barre* to warm up and loosen the hip joint and increase the turnout of the legs. *Rond de jambe à terre* may be done in two ways:

a circling of the leg in an outward direction (called *"rond de jambe en de hors")* or in an inward direction (called *"rond de jambe en de dans").* In either case, the extended or working leg makes a perfect semicircle on the floor. A combined series of *en de hors* and *en de dans ronds de jambe* are usually done at the *barre*, the dancer beginning with *rond de jambe en de hors*.

*En de hors* — standing with the heels together in first position, the dancer slides one foot forward along the floor, lifting the heel as the leg and foot extend fully to the front. Both remain extended as the foot is swept along the floor through second position to the back. The foot is then brought forward again as the heel lowers into first position. (The exercise is completed when the foot continues forward to the fully extended position front.) When done consecutively, *ronds de jambe* are usually preceded by a *préparation* in which the foot is brought front, then side. The dancer pauses and carries the leg to the back before starting the exercise.

*Rond de jambe en de dans* is done in exactly the same way except that the foot begins by brushing to the back.

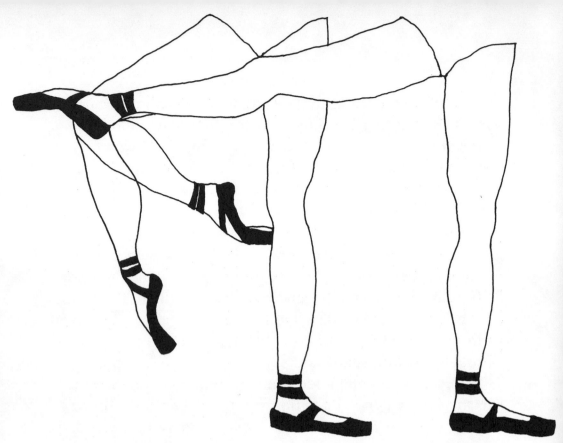

**Rond de jambe en l'air** — *(rahn due zhamb ahm LEHR)*
*Rond de jambe en l'air* means "a *rond de jambe* in the air."
It is an exercise done at the *barre* and in the center to warm
up and loosen the knee joint. Standing on one leg, the
dancer brushes the other leg off the ground directly to the
side. The foot of the extended leg then describes an oval in
the air, returning to and from the extended position by way
of the standing leg. The height of the *rond de jambe* may
vary depending upon the tempo of the music but should
never exceed hip level. The entire movement of the leg
must come from below the knee. The movement is also
uneven, meaning that the leg must make the oval very
quickly, showing off the extended position. On stage, women
do *ronds de jambe* on *pointe,* while men often jump into the
air and execute a double *rond de jambe* before landing.

116

**Rond de jambe, grand** — *(grahn rahn duh ZHAMB)*
*Grand rond de jambe* means "a large circular movement of the leg." It is used to describe any semicircular movement of the extended leg, either back to front or front to back. It differs from the *rond de jambe à terre* in that the leg does not go through first position. The movement may also be done in the air.

**Royal Ballet** — The Royal Ballet is England's major ballet company. It is based at the Royal Opera House in London's Covent Garden, but tours the world extensively. It was originally known as the Sadler's Wells Ballet, founded by Dame Nanette De Valois in 1926. It began modestly but expanded rapidly with the arrival of ballerina Alicia Markova and choreographer Frederick Ashton. A young girl of fifteen named Margot Fonteyn appeared soon after and rose swiftly to become the company's greatest star.

The Second World War sent Sadler's Wells on tour. Despite the difficulties of war, it forged bravely ahead adding many new works by Frederick Ashton, including *Les Patineurs* and *Nocturne,* to a repertoire which was already steeped in the classics, such as *Giselle, Swan Lake* and *Sleeping Beauty.*

On April 6, 1946, a second company was formed, a group designed to train young dancers for the senior company. They merged ten years later and the new company was called, by order of the Royal charter, the Royal Ballet. At the same time a school was formed, providing a set system for the training of dancers from beginning to professional levels.

The company has a very understated and elegant style, with a *corps de ballet* known for its precision of both line and movement. Some of the world's greatest dancers have worked with the company including Rudolf Nureyev, Margot Fonteyn, Anthony Dowell, Antoinette Sibley, Carla Fracci and others. In the days of increasingly acrobatic and athletic dancing, when companies lose sight of the fact that ballet is art and *not* sport, it is refreshing to know that the quiet elegance of the Royal Ballet remains. The company is currently under the direction of Kenneth Macmillan.

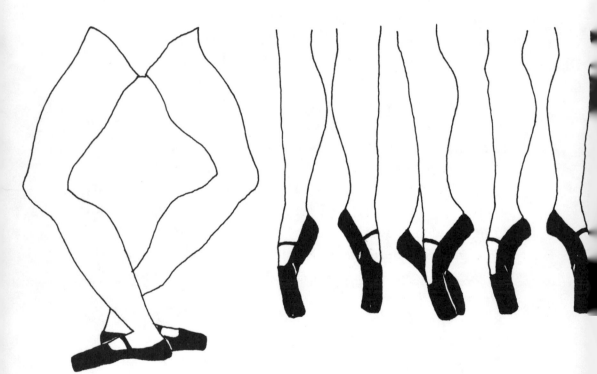

**Royale** — *(rwah-YAL) Royale* means "royal" and is used to describe a beaten *changement*. From the fifth position, the dancer jumps into the air, beats the calves of the legs together, then changes the position of the feet before landing. The *royale* was invented by Louis XIV of France who was too fat and out-of-shape to execute the more difficult *entrechat-quatre. (*see *Entrechat-quatre.)*

**Sauté —** *(soh-TAY)* *Sauté* means "jumped." When any position or movement is followed by the word *sauté,* it means that action must be performed while jumping into the air, i.e., *arabesque sauté, echappé sauté.*

**Sauté de basque —** *(soh-TAY duh BASK)* *Sauté de basque* means "a jump characteristic of the Basque people." It is a traveling step in which the dancer executes one or two turns in the air with the foot of one leg attached to the knee of the other.

**Sauté de chat —** *(soh-TAY duh SHAT)* *Sauté de chat* means "a cat's jump." It is a spectacular leaping action. It is used many times by dancers to "leap into the wings" at the end of a segment. Beginning with a *préparation* step or running start, the dancer rises swiftly off the ground, stretching one leg to the front, the other to the back. While in the air, the dancer bends the front leg at the knee then thrusts it straight again, does a split in the air and lands on the front leg in *demi-plié* while the back leg remains extended with straight knee.

**Serré —** *(seh-RAY)* *Serré* means "tight" or "closed." Always done either on *pointe* or *demi-pointe*, the toes of one foot make a series of rapid little beats or taps against the raised heel of the other.

**Sissone —** *(see-SOHN)* *Sissone* is named for the originator of the step. Basically, it is a jump from two feet, landing onto one. There are two major types of *sissone, ouverte* ("open") and *fermée* ("closed"). The *sissone ouverte* means that upon landing on one foot, the second foot remains extended in the air. *Fermée,* on the other hand, means that upon landing the second foot closes immediately.

**Sleeping Beauty** — *Sleeping Beauty* was first produced in 1890 in St. Petersburg, Russia, choreographed by Marius Petipa, with music by Peter Tchaikovsky. The ballet is made up of a Prologue and three Acts (although the Prologue is long and elaborate enough to be considered an act in itself). The *Sleeping Beauty* ballet is a retelling of the famous tale of Sleeping Beauty, a story concerning a beautiful princess who, doomed to fall asleep on her sixteenth birthday for a hundred years, is awakened by the kiss of a handsome prince and lives "happily ever after." It remains, to this day, one of ballet's most enchanting works.

The *Sleeping Beauty* opens in the mythical kingdom of King Florestan XXIV, whose wife has just given birth to a daughter, the princess Aurora. It is her christening day and all the fairy godmothers, including the most beautiful and powerful Lilac fairy, are in attendance. Everything is going smoothly, when a page comes in to report that the king and queen have forgotten to invite the wicked fairy, Caraboose. A moment later, the black coach carrying Caraboose arrives on the scene. She decrees that Aurora will live until her sixteenth birthday, whereupon she will prick her finger and die. The Lilac fairy quickly intercedes. She tells the family that while the curse may not be removed, it may be softened somewhat — that instead of dying, the princess will sleep for a hundred years. The king and queen are as grateful as can be expected under the circumstances and the guests depart.

Act I opens with Aurora's sixteenth birthday party. Aurora graciously dances with four different suitors, each vying for her hand, presenting her with roses and kisses, a dance which has become known as the famous *Rose Adagio*.

The dancing and merriment continue as the wicked Caraboose sneaks in, bearing in her hand a strange gift for Aurora. Aurora takes the gift. To everyone's horror, she pricks her finger and falls asleep. Suddenly, the Lilac fairy appears and orders the princess to be taken upstairs to her bedroom, then makes everyone fall asleep, as she covers the palace with thick foliage to hide it from the rest of the country.

Act II takes place in a forest where Prince Florimund is having a perfectly boring time hunting with his friends. He is visited by the Lilac fairy who tells him of the princess and the hidden castle. Florimund is skeptical at first but when the Lilac fairy causes a vision of Aurora to appear, he falls in love at once and begs the Lilac fairy to lead him to the palace. As the act ends, the two are seen stepping into a magical boat, gliding across the lake.

In the first part of Act III, the Lilac fairy is seen leading Florimund to the princess' bedroom. He kneels at her side, kisses her. And she awakes in his arms.

The ballet concludes with Aurora's wedding celebration. There are many dances including the famous *Bluebird pas de deux,* with a Bluebird and his enchanted princess, all reflecting the joy and happiness of the occasion.

**Soloist —** A soloist is a dancer of either sex who is the second highest ranking member of any ballet company. The secondary roles in classical ballet are given to the soloist.

**Soubresant** — *(soo-bruh—SOH) Soubresant* means "sudden spring" or "bound." Starting from fifth position, the dancer springs either forward or backward into the air, bringing the upper body forward and extending the palms to the audience. The legs also come slightly forward, but remain together in fifth position, one foot hiding the other. The body is straightened and the dancer lands in fifth position in *demi-plié* without changing the relationship of the feet. *Soubresants* may also be done on *pointe* and *demi-pointe*.

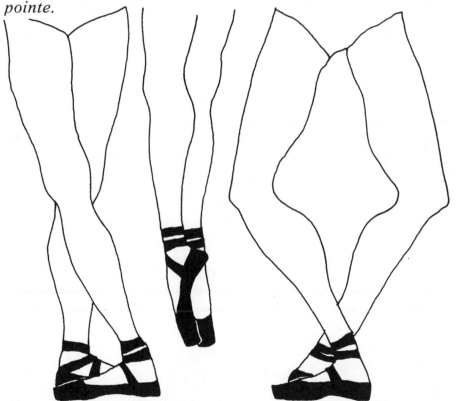

**Soutenu en tournant** — *(soo-ten-new ahn toor-NAHn) Soutenu en tournant* means "sustained in turning." There are two types of *soutenu en tournant: en de hors* ("outward turn") or *en de dans* ("inward turn").

*En de hors* — the dancer crosses the right foot in front of the left, rising to *demi* or full *pointe.* The body then makes a complete turn with the legs together, closing in fifth position *demi-plié* with the left foot in front. The turn may be done to the other side as well, crossing the left foot in front of the right.

*En de dans* — this turn is the same as the *en de hors* except that one foot crosses behind the other. Both *en de hors* and *en de dans soutenus* are usually preceded by a *dégagé. (*see *Dégagé.)*

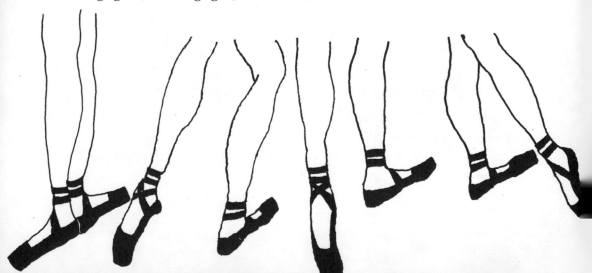

**Spotting** — *Spotting* or "head movement," as it is sometimes called, is the sharp, rhythmical snapping of the head made by the dancer while turning. It not only prevents dizziness but gives direction, clarity and speed to the turns as well. Before beginning the turn, the dancer chooses and focuses upon a "spot" — a fixed object usually some distance away (such as one of the "exit" signs at the back of the theater). While the body turns, the head and eyes are the last to leave but the first to return to the "spot" as the turn is completed. When turning steps are done while traveling across stage, the dancer "spots" in the direction to which he or she is turning.

**Stravinsky, Igor** — *(stra-VIN-skee)* Born in Russia in 1881, Stravinsky was a composer whose complex music has been used as the basis for many well known modern ballets. Until his death just a few years ago, he and modern choreographer George Balanchine of New York City Ballet worked closely together to create some forty ballets. Among his most famous works are: *Petrouchka, Firebird, Rite of Spring* and *Agon.* (see *Agon, Balanchine.*)

**Stretches —** Stretches are exercises which are done either in or out of class to keep the muscles as loose and limber as possible. They include splits, front and back, back bends, sitting like a frog on the stomach, lying on the back and bringing the legs up over the head, touching the toes, sliding the legs out along the *barre* and countless others which dancers manage to dream up for themselves.

**Supporting or Standing Leg —** This term is used to describe the leg upon which the dancer stands or from which he jumps while executing any step or pose.

**Swan Lake** — *Swan Lake* was first choreographed by Jules Reisinger, with music by Peter I. Tchaikovsky in Moscow in 1877. While this version was fairly successful, most *Swan Lakes* produced today are based on the choreography of Marius Petipa (Acts I and III) and Lev Ivanov (Acts II and IV) who restaged the ballet in 1895. The story of the full length version is as follows:

Prince Seigfried is having a somewhat rowdy twenty-first birthday party with several of his friends. His mother walks in and is dismayed by his carefree behavior. She announces that the prince is to be married immediately and must choose his bride from among several princesses who will be in attendance at a ball to be held the following night. Upset at his mother's decree and noticing some swans flying overhead, Seigfried and his friends decide to stop the party and go hunting by the lake.

Act II begins when the hunters arrive by the lake and notice the swans have gathered there. Seigfried orders his men to take up their hunting positions. All of a sudden something attracts his attention and causes him to stop and hide nearby. Out of the clearing walks a beautiful creature, part woman, part bird, dressed in pure white with the face and body of a woman, but with a head framed with feathers and the movements of a swan. The prince steps forward and gently asks the trembling creature her name. In mime, she tells him that she is Odette, queen of the Swans, currently under the spell of the evil magician, Von Rothbart. He has transformed her into a swan, allowing her to be human just between the hours of midnight and dawn. Only a pledge of marriage and eternal devotion can break the spell.

Seigfried falls immediately in love. He promises to marry her. Suddenly, Von Rothbart appears to take her away. Seigfried raises his crossbow to kill the evil Von Rothbart but Odette stops him. Von Rothbart leaves angrily.

The prince then tells Odette of the ball to be held in his honor and begs her to attend. She will not and warns Seigfried that Von Rothbart may somehow try to deceive him into breaking his vow. The two leave the glade together. The Act ends with a beautiful *Adagio*, a dance of love between Seigfried and Odette and a dance of the swans. As dawn approaches, the lovers sadly part.

In Act III, the guests have arrived for the birthday ball. Seigfried, preoccupied with thoughts of Odette, dances indifferently with each of the princesses. Suddenly the music crashes and Von Rothbart, (disguised as a knight) and his daughter Odile enter the room. Despite her black dress, Seigfried believes that she is really Odette and begins to dance with her, in what is now known as the *Black Swan Pas de Deux*. Outside the window, Odette is frantically trying to catch Seigfried's attention but he is so overwhelmed by Odile's charms that he does not even notice Odette.

When the dance is finished (and still convinced that Odile is Odette) Seigfried swears his love and eternal devotion. Triumphantly, Von Rothbart and Odile leave the room. Only then does Seigfried see Odette at the window. Realizing at last that he has been duped, Seigfried falls in despair to the floor.

In the fourth act, Seigfried rushes back to the lake, where the despondent Odette is trying to kill herself. She explains that with his vow of love to Odile, they may never be united. She plunges headlong into the lake. Seigfried soon follows. As they are at last joined together in triumphant love, the spell of Von Rothbart is broken. When dawn comes up, Odette and Seigfried are seen gliding on a boat to a new world of love and happiness.

**Sylphides, Les** — *Les Sylphides* was choreographed by Michel Fokine for Diaghilev's Ballets Russes in Paris in 1909. One year before, he had choreographed a somewhat different version called *Chopiniana*, which was danced by the Russian Imperial Ballet in St. Petersburg. The Bolshoi and Royal Danish Ballets use the later version but still call the ballet "*Chopiniana.*"

*Les Sylphides* is named for a famous romantic ballet, *La Syphide,* since the dancers are dressed in the long, flowing skirts similar to the one used by Maria Taglioni in *La Sylphide.* The ballet consists of a series of dances done to the nocturnes, waltzes and mazurkas of Frédéric Chopin and is usually set in a moonlit forest glade. Having no story or plot, *Les Sylphides* is a lovely display of dances done in the Romantic style. It is often called a *ballet blanc* or "white ballet" because it is a ballet in which all the women are dressed in white.

# T

**Tchaikovsky, Peter I.** — *(chai-COUGH-skee)* Peter Tchaikovsky was a Russian born composer who lived from 1840 to 1893. His music inspired many of the classical ballets we see today. *Swan Lake, Sleeping Beauty* and *The Nutcracker* are but three of his most famous works.

**Temps du cuisse —** *(tahn duh KWEES) Temps de cuisse* means "thigh movement." It is a step from the fifth position in which one foot is picked up and placed sharply in front or in back of the other followed by a small *sissone fermée.* (*Sissone fermée* is a jump from two feet landing onto one, the second foot closing immediately upon landing.) *Temps de cuisse* is done traveling slightly forward or back.

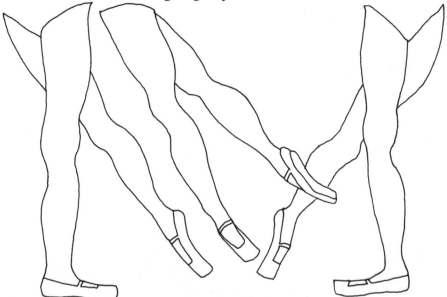

**Temps de flèche —** *(tahn duh FLESH) Temps de flèche* means "step of the arrow." The step is called *temps de flèche* because one leg acts as a bow, the other as an arrow. The dancer swiftly raises one leg (the bow) into the air to the front, bends the leg at the knee and extends it to the back. The second leg (the arrow) "shoots" to the front at the same time. *Temps de flèche* may also be done by executing two *grand battements,* one on each leg, in rapid succession. The second *grand battement* must occur before the first one is finished causing the legs to pass each other in the air. On Broadway, this step is called a "hitchkick."

**Temps levé** — *(tahn luh-VAY) Temps levé* means "a raising movement." It is a hop from one foot, in any position, i.e., *temps levé en arabesque, en attitude,* etc.

**Temps de poisson** — *(tahn duh pwah-SOHn) Temps de poisson* means "step of the fish." The dancer springs into the air, raising the arms over the head and arching the back. The legs which are held together and crossed, shoot behind the dancer, forming, as it were, a fish's tail. The landing is made on the underneath leg, while the top leg remains extended to the back. The dancer usually completes the step by brushing the extended leg to the front and executing an *assemblé.* (see *Assemblé.)*

**Tendu** — *(tahn-DEW)* *Tendu* means "stretched." It usually refers to the foot being stretched or held in a fully stretched position, as in *battement tendu*.

**Terre, à** — *(ah TEHR)* *A terre* means "on the ground." It is used to indicate either the entire base of the foot is to remain on the floor or that when a foot is extended to a certain position, the toes are to remain on the floor. *Arabesque à terre* is one example.

**Terre à terre** — *(tehr ah TEHR) Terre à terre* means "on the ground." It is used to indicate that a step must be executed with the feet on or close to the ground. Any dancer who lacks height in jumps is said to be a *terre à terre dancer.*

**Tour** — *(toor) Tour* means "turn." It means any turn of the body.

**Tour en l'air** — *(toor ahn LEHR) Tour en l'air* means "a turn in the air." From a *demi-plié* position (usually fifth) the body is shot up into the air and makes a 360° turn before landing. When two turns are made in the air, it is called a double *tour* — one of the most important steps in the male dancer's vocabulary. The dancer may land from the *tour* in a number of different positions including: fifth, one leg extended to the side, *arabesque* or onto one knee.

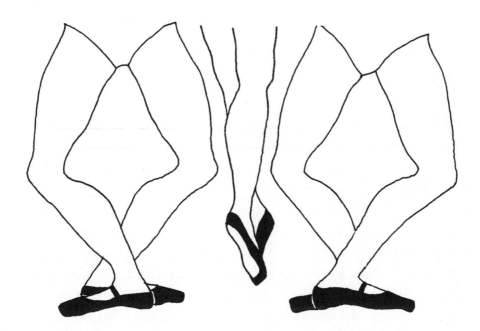

**Tournant, en** — *(ahn toor-NAHN) En tournant* means "turning." It is used to indicate that the body must turn while performing any given step, as in *assemblé en tournant*.

**Turnout** — All ballet technique is based on the turnout of the feet and legs. It is a rotation outward of the entire leg to a 90° position. The inside of the thigh is brought forward and the knee is made to face out to the side. Turnout gives the dancer complete mobility and control of the legs, and the ability to move freely in any direction. In addition, when the feet are turned out, the dancer has more of a base upon which to stand. It comes in part from certain fencing positions and from the fact that men in the seventeenth century (when *turnout* was first developed) wore bucket top boots or boots which opened out at the top. The only way to move easily in these boots was by turning out the legs.

**Tutu** — *(too-TOO)* A skirt worn by the female dancer. The romantic *tutu* comes down below the calf. Later *tutus* were shortened, jutting straight out from the hips.

# U V

**Variation** — Any solo dance, and the third section of a *grand pas de deux*.

**Villella, Edward** — Edward Villella is one of America's best dancers. His strong and virile manner has done much to establish the male dancer as a masculine and athletic type and not as a "sissy," as was once supposed. He was born on Long Island in 1936 and began his training with the School of American Ballet at age ten. Five years later, however, he was forced by his family to quit dancing in order to attend college, but was able to resume his career upon graduation and joined New York City Ballet in 1957. Villella has been there ever since, dancing the ballets of George Balanchine and Jerome Robbins, most notably *Interplay, Symphony in C, Agon* and his greatest role, the lead in *The Prodigal Son.* In addition, he has made numerous television appearances, including several which have tried to show the similarities between ballet and sport. Villella's inspiration and example have encouraged many young American boys to take up dancing.

# WXYZ

**Warm-up Exercises** — Before every performance and usually before a class, one may see a dancer haphazardly performing a mixture of *tendues, pliés, relevés,* splits, backbends, etc. to quickly warm up and prepare the muscles for what lies ahead. These warm-up exercises vary from dancer to dancer, each having learned from personal experience what works best for his or her own body. To quicken the "warm-up" process, the dancers may put several layers of woolen stockings and sweaters over their tights or costumes, removing them gradually while in class or tossing them quickly aside before going on stage.

**Working Leg** — The leg which extends or performs the movement while standing on the other leg.

Although this is his first children's book, EVAN JAFFE is an expert on ballet. Mr. Jaffe grew up in Denver, Colorado, and after studying ballet in New York City, he joined the ranks of *Ballet Western Reserve* in Youngstown, Ohio, a professional company with whom he danced and taught. At the present, he has returned to New York to complete his academic studies at Columbia University while continuing to pursue his interest in dance.

PHYLLIS LERNER has done illustration work for various magazines, designed textiles for a well-known pattern company and has designed brochures and clothing for different firms in New York City. A native of the city, Ms. Lerner received a B.F.A. in Media Arts from the School of Visual Arts. She is currently working for the *Village Voice* and doing free-lance illustration and design.

devant

croisé devant

corps de ballet  corps de ballet